A~MANDA~ B~ROOK~ C~ELAR'S~

Of a not so civil war

Amanda Brook Celar

authorHOUSE®

AuthorHouse™ UK
1663 Liberty Drive
Bloomington, IN 47403 USA
www.authorhouse.co.uk
Phone: 0800.197.4150

Published by AuthorHouse 04/22/2016

ISBN: 978-1-5246-3211-3 (sc)
ISBN: 978-1-5246-3210-6 (e)

In memory of

Josip Reihl-Kir   Franjo Cvetković   Srbobran Krnjulac

For those that lost their lives or sanity in the fight
against racism and the defence of their homes
and homeland and for all those in exile.

Acknowledgements

Ilija Čelar, for his incredible support, patience, advice, and love.

Alec Ashby, Mary Connelly, Marion Joli, Zorica Jovanović, Dragica Tadić-Papanikola, Bill Sharpe, Susan Walton and Goran 'jingo the kid' Senic, for their innate common sense and invaluable assistance.

Jude and Ken Winters: for their printing, postal services and unconditional support.

CHAPTERS

CHAPTER ONE

As the plane banked left on its final approach to Schiphol airport in Holland, I saw rows and rows of neatly shaped fields, as symmetrical and ordered as if they had been precisely measured. I was later told that indeed they had and that this was a significant point of pride for their owners.

I felt no fear or dread, well, perhaps a little apprehension. I was here to testify at the ICTY or, 'The International Criminal Tribunal for the former Yugoslavia,' in The Hague. I had been approached by members of a defence team in 2014 asking if I were willing to testify at the trial of a Serbian politician Goran Hadzic. He had been President of the Republic of Serbian Krajina for a period during the civil war. I had never met him, and most of my prepared statement was based on the articles I had written in 1991 and to various other documents of the time. Born and bred an English woman I was the only person that they could trace, who could be considered neutral and had witnessed events in the region before, during and after the conflict there. All I had to do was to remember, in detail, what had happened some 27 years ago during the times I spent in Baranja and Croatia in the North of the former Yugoslavia. Well, how easy was that!

Except that, I had buried that period of my life either consciously or subconsciously trying to erase it from my memory. So many friends dead, so many lost to new countries and new nationalities, so much despair and hopelessness at what was considered, by most of them, a bitter defeat and betrayal.

I think some of these recollections could be compared to childhood memories; are they one's own or were you told about them by a parent or other members of your family? It was important to be factual and truthful, and I had agonized over some of these memories.

My first flight to Amsterdam in 1987 had been for an entirely different reason. My marriage of 21 years was broken beyond repair. There was I, an English woman abroad at the ripe old age of 43 and with a reasonable divorce settlement agreed upon, I was off to seek my fortune. I had worked hard with a strict fitness regime to prepare for this wonderful new life. And so now, at around 55kg, a five-foot-two, not unattractive blonde, I set off on the 'great adventure', choosing the Netherlands as my first destination. I quickly found myself an apartment in Amsterdam. Joined a local fitness club, where I hoped to shed a few more pounds, and set about making new friends. In these early days, I sometimes had the strangest sensation that I was watching myself, a spectator to the decision making. I had no particular plans for the future and had no inclination to make any.

How strange is fate? My hairdresser was running late and asked me if I could return in another half an hour, so I decided to go and buy my daily paper and visit my usual café, the Number Nine in Legmeerstraat. I was planning to fly to visit some friends in Cumbria in the North of England but had not decided on a date. Then on that fateful day in early November, I met the love of my life, Ilija Čelar! Initially, our first encounter actually didn't go very well although as soon as I saw him, I felt an intense attraction. Slim, about 5ft 9 tall, fair-haired and handsome, and mid-thirties I thought, he was sitting at an adjacent table with some companions. We made eye contact, and I shifted my gaze, but he continued to look at me so directly and without any sign of embarrassment that I just stared back.

He leant over and asked in English if he could have a light for his cigarette. Handing him my lighter, I realized that I was fervently hoping he would talk to me! I had no idea what I would say if he did, flirting doesn't come easily to me. I had worked with men most of my working life and had always tried to stay pretty matter-of-fact and to deflect or ignore any advances. He looked at me intently and told me that since I was reading an English newspaper he assumed I was English and could he join me for a minute? Taking a seat opposite to me and after glancing at my paper, he looked up and smiled at me. I said the first thing that came into my head which was, 'are you, Russian?' I had never met anyone from Russia and didn't know why I said it. My problem is that when I am nervous, I begin to talk non-stop without any real idea of what I am saying, rudely coined by one of my brothers as verbal diarrhoea. A pair of beautiful grey eyes looked at me and said, 'no, I am Serbian.' To my shame I had no idea where Serbia was, he realized this and quickly added, 'Yugoslavia.' Now on firmer ground, I said confidently, 'Ah yes, you had a great President called Tito who was a friend of our Prime Minister Winston Churchill.' His response changed everything. 'Tito was a bastard' he said, 'and Churchill an even bigger one.' I swiftly moved back to reading my newspaper and felt slightly ruffled by what I thought was his arrogance and the conversation went no further.

And then I heard him call out to the coffee bar owner, 'Bruno, do you have a pen, please? I want to take down this lovely lady's address and telephone number.' I was appalled to see most other patrons of the café swivelling their seats to study both of us. Ilija said, 'do you have any English books I could borrow, please? I need to improve my English, and it would be so kind of you if you could.' The charm worked, and I promised to look him out some reading material and left him reading my newspaper. I was to learn that he was a sweet, gentle person, given to moments of showing off to impress!

A little later in the day, barefooted, I answered a knock on the door to find Ilija standing there with a large bunch of flowers clutched in his hand. He looked down at me and said, 'you are much smaller than I thought you were!' To which I responded, 'have you got the right person?' The actual reason for his confusion was that I usually wore very high heels! I was totally nonplussed, and as he followed me into the flat, I invited him to sit down while I made us a drink. I disappeared into my little kitchen and made a pot of Ceylon tea, put dainty cups and saucers, sugar bowl and milk jug on a tray and then I just froze. Afterwards, Ilija told me that he had almost given up waiting and was thinking about leaving when I finally appeared with the tea. He was sitting on one of the two sofas; he sat a little awkwardly, and I immediately realized that he was just as nervous as I was. I poured the tea and added milk. Because I at this stage didn't realize that drinking tea with milk is not a Serbian habit. In all probability, because herb tea is a more popular one than Indian or Ceylon, or, Russian as Serbians seem to refer to it. He hid his revulsion and appeared to empty most of the sugar bowl into his cup. I sat opposite to him and as my eyes met his I again felt almost mesmerized by his gaze. I believe that the eyes mirror the soul and felt completely comfortable to be here, alone in a big city, with a stranger I had only just met.

We chatted, and I soon discovered what an interesting person he is. I can ask him absolutely anything. About such diverse subjects as astronomy, geography, the Bible, history, biology, Greek mythology, music, science, maths, Latin, Greek, or literature for he is very well read. He also studies languages for fun! However, I was to learn that this perfection does not extend to include anything remotely connected to practical skills. He once spent ages looking for a place to fill with hydraulic, brake fluid for the handbrake of our little Yugo car until I told him it was cable operated! And he always gets mad the way they sell so many faulty screws that will not hold curtain rails up in place! He is never happier than when he has 'his nose in a book'. As the children of a farmer, these involved taking some of their stock to graze on the common land. Ilija, careless of everything, would read his book while his charges wandered far away. Fortunately, his mother recognized and encouraged his love of books and eagerness for knowledge, but his siblings just thought it grossly unfair when they had to take on his chores in addition to their own.

As a three-year-old, Ilija had often followed his 7-year-old sister into the classroom of her elderly, Jewish teacher, David Ashner, in Jagodnjak primary school. With the help of not only the Serbian villagers but the ethnic Germans too, Ashner's family had somehow survived the Holocaust and was now a much-loved mentor. He too recognized Ilija's thirst for knowledge, and so began Ilija's education.

Ashner had an enormous collection of books, quite unusual for that time and place and Ilija was allowed to wander in this library whenever he wished. The teacher and his wife grew very fond of him, feeding him, encouraging him, teaching him mathematics, reading, writing and the Cyrillic alphabet all from the age of three. He regularly took him to a local café and stood him up on a table. From here Ilija would either read a Cyrillic newspaper aloud to the patrons or solve simple, multiplication or subtraction problems set by Ashner. Ilija looked forward to these performances because he always got some chocolate from the patrons as a reward. When Ilija was six Ashner approached his parents, Risto, and Vida and made a proposal to them. He and his family were going to move to America and would Risto, and Vida allow them to adopt Ilija? He explained that he regarded him as a child prodigy with prodigious talent. They would pay for the finest schools in helping to him to achieve his real potential. Ilija parents turned him down flat, and the Ashner family left the following year. Ilija clearly remembers his library, and that he had a gramophone, the first Ilija had ever seen. He recalls what sadness he felt, the morning his father told him that the Ashner family had gone and that he shouldn't go to their house anymore. I don't know, even after all this time together, whether he resents that missed opportunity and I suppose neither does he. Nothing has quelled his desire for knowledge and a willingness to share it. I regret that Ilija didn't turn to the teaching profession too. He would have made an excellent tutor. He is no intellectual snob nor know- it- all and loves to debate and share his knowledge with others!

Now, in those first halcyon days, careless of everything else we just enjoyed discovering things about each other. He now came every day to see me and then one day he simply picked me up carrying me into the bedroom, and I didn't even think about kicking or screaming. There, we stayed for the next four days with the odd break for bathing and eating. I knew I was passionately in love with this extraordinary man, an amazing and tender lover, gentle and kind who fed me segments of orange and other small pieces of fruit because he believed I was anorexic.

And he was probably right, for I was losing weight at the rate of a kilogram a week. I ate only enough calories to equal those I would burn at the aerobics club. Like some other women in my position, being middle-aged with one failed marriage had affected my sense of self-worth and to become slim seemed to be the panacea. My weight had plummeted to around 49kg, but I still thought I needed to lose more until that is, I met Ilija. We agreed that he would give up his flat and move in with me which only left the decisions regarding his imminent departure to Cape Town and my return to the UK for the coming Christmas holiday. However, separation now just wasn't an option, and so each of our previous plans was abandoned, and we spent Christmas together in our little flat in Amsterdam. Ilija bought a small Christmas tree, and I made a Christmas pudding in a ceramic plant pot!

We began a passionate love affair. I knew the recklessness of it and that I was ricocheting from a long-term relationship into a crazy love affair with a man 12 years my junior. But absolutely nothing mattered to me, and I fell deeply in love with someone who was endlessly fascinating and an attentive and caring lover. For his part, Ilija told me that he would like to settle down with me. That he had spent many years travelling and now wanted us to make our lives together, wherever we decided that should be. But he also thought that we should take time over our decisions, there was no cause to hurry. I was bombarded with phone calls from concerned friends, even employees of our company and family in England and Wales. I did the decent thing and revealed where my company car, a red Porsche 924 was garaged and sent my resignation as a director of the company. I had made my decision.

My closest friend Jude simply got on a plane and arrived on the doorstep of our Amsterdam apartment to see if I had completely lost my mind or what? The 'or what' satisfied her. She met Ilija, liked him and although extremely anxious about my lack of plans for the future; she happily returned home to report back, to those that I cared about, that I was fine. My mother informed me in her telephone call of the following evening that I wasn't to worry about gossip. She had told her friends at the church that I was going through the menopause and was perfectly fine other than that. My father, on the other hand, truthfully admitted that he was utterly confused by my behaviour. However, since I was old enough to make my such choices they would just offer support if I needed or asked for it. I had not confided in my parents my reasons for leaving my first husband; I couldn't bear to talk about it and only explained that the marriage was over. I then recalled an unusual event in my life when I was a new bride aged 22. I was strolling, with my then mother-in-law, across a fairground near Swansea in South Wales. We stepped inside a little fortune-teller's tent and for the very first and last time in my life I had my fortune told. Holding my hand and peering intently at my palm, all I can remember is the woman making a very strange prediction. She said 'you will not stay married to this man, you will marry another and end your days across the seas.' We paid her and left, and my mother-in-law was furious at her predictions, but I remember telling her not to worry because she probably told everyone the same thing. I wonder if she did.

And now Ilija and I began to get to know each other. I was to learn that he hated shopping but adored clothes. And he had an addiction! Ilija has an enormous collection of colognes! He is also a talented, classical guitarist and is a lover of Flamenco. The music of Ravel, Bach, Beethoven and Tchaikovsky besides many other composers is an important part of his life. He owned a vast collection of music cassettes from the sixties- on including The Doors, Rolling Stones, Mamas and Papas, Cockney Rebels, Leonard Cohen and Janice Joplin to name but a few. We enjoyed the same music then! He is a very tolerant, non-judgemental friend, generous with his time and is an attentive listener. Slow to anger and quick to forgive, in fact, the complete opposite to me! Most of the time he rescues me from situations where I am positively floundering, occasionally he doesn't.

One evening we invited some Dutch, musician friends of Ilija's for dinner. A wonderfully, colourful and lively bunch they came with, armfuls of flowers and embraced us both warmly. One of them called Freddy, 'the philosopher,' left me a little startled as he informed me that, 'as long as I can not get pregnant, I can not give birth.' I looked over to Ilija, who had a broad grin on his face. As we enjoyed our coffee, Freddy asked me if I smoked. 'Yes,' I replied. 'No, she doesn't,' interjected Ilija. I turned to argue this point declaring that indeed I did when, out of the corner of my eye, I saw the hashish pipe coming out of Freddy's bag. Ilija smiled, and they all looked a little incredulous as I told them I had never seen any drugs before in my life let alone smoked any. I felt very unworldly, and a little out of my depth, and neither of us accepted the proffered pipe. One of these friends worked in publishing, and they began a lively debate about the books of Herman Hesse. Freddy put away his pipe and told me how much he was looking forward to some English cooking.

I took the hint and disappeared into our little kitchen to begin serving dinner to our friends. I had agonized somewhat over the menu. So I had made a huge lasagne, salad and there were fresh strawberries for dessert, which I thought would be pretty safe since I had no idea of the preferences of these new friends of mine. Ilija has always been bemused by our English cuisine, especially, in his view, our strange habit of pouring soup (to be precise gravy) over our food. I served sweet corn as a starter. I had even bought some of those special tiny forks and served them with a little dish of melted butter. Ilija just stared at the corn! Whispering in his ear, I asked if he knew what it was and that he should sprinkle some salt and butter over it. He just said quietly 'yes, I know what it is.' Months later, as we drove through the Yugoslavian countryside, I saw hundreds of sweetcorn cobs piled high in small wooden buildings they call 'chardak.' The sweetcorn was livestock fodder, and then I understood his reaction to my starter speciality. When my mother saw the chardaks in 1988, on her first visit to Osijek from England, she declared that there must be a lot of millionaires living there because a single cob at home in England cost £1.

Another of our regular visitors was Jovan, a tall, dark-haired, gaunt Serbian, who had been a political prisoner of the Communist regime in Yugoslavia. He seemed to have an aimless life but, told us he could never return to his homeland, even though he had a wife and child there. He was a sad and lonely figure, and there were other friends of ours, who seemed to live this nomadic life. I now concluded that even though my initial plans had been to roam Europe for a few years unless I had a purpose for such travel, I wasn't going to enjoy being an eternal tourist. And in light of this, Ilija and I now seriously discussed our future together. Neither of us felt that we wanted to make our home here, in the Netherlands, delightful country that it is.

Ilija had travelled throughout Europe after he had completed his obligatory period of service in the J.N.A (Yugoslavian National Army) and he had an excellent job offer from a company in South Africa. I didn't want to live there because I feared what the future held as the country emerged from its apartheid past. Ilija wasn't keen to go to the UK. He now suggested that we could probably be very contented, or to use Ilija's favourite expression, 'as happy as Larry,' in his beautiful country. Perhaps, for this reason, we should go and visit his family to see how we felt.

I knew very little about Yugoslavia, and what little I did know, I had learned from my brother Simon. As a student, he had backpacked there and had caused some consternation within the family because he had only just escaped by a day or so from the catastrophic earthquake in Skopje in 1963. It had killed over a thousand people and devastated the city. On his return, he told us at length how he had been thrilled by the diversity of the country, its peoples, and geography and by a beautiful language script called Cyrillic. He had not given me the impression that the Communist regime in Yugoslavia was remotely Stalinist, and I was, therefore, not at all concerned. I have never shied away from either a new experience or challenge and so at the age of 43 I was off on an even greater adventure. However, I had no intention of making any firm plans to either live there or, to marry Ilija.

CHAPTER TWO

And so in early January 1988, Ilija and I and nine large suitcases arrived at Belgrade airport. We were greeted by a man who I came to respect, love and admire and who was to become my brother-in-law or, in the Serbo/Croat language, shogor. Franjo Kerovec enveloped me in an enormous bear hug as we came into the arrivals hall. 'Welcome, welcome, I speak English, welcome! Come! Come! Here is a car!' He was about the same height as Ilija, but much more powerfully built. With greying hair and bright blue eyes, that twinkled with an air of devilment! Behind Franjo, were four other faces all smiling, all hugging and kissing us. Boban, a family friend, was a tall, lean, good-looking man his sixties. His wife Mina was almost as tall, and I thought she would smother me as she hugged and kissed me! Meanwhile, Ilija had been lifted bodily into the air by one of the two young men who I later discovered were Franjo's nephews, Petar, and Mikhail.

They had arrived in two cars, but we quickly realized we needed to hire another to accommodate all our baggage. We hired an Opel, which was to severely, test Franjo's driving ability and patience because this dear man had never driven a car with a reverse stick-shift that needed to be raised upwards to work. And so, unable to engage reverse gear, after we overshot our turning off the highway on our way to our destination, Franjo simply did a circuit of a nearby field. Ilija had no idea, and it hadn't occurred to either of them to ask a woman if she knew how to put the car into reverse. I felt it unwise so early in my relationship with my new shogor to outrage his sensibilities, and so I kept quiet. And our little convoy must have seemed a very strange sight as three cars did a complete circuit of the field before resuming their journey. We stopped for coffee shortly afterwards, and there was a furious 3-way conversation between drivers.

I was to get used to these explosive outbursts that always included some extravagant arm waving, table thumping and usually, finally, hugs and laughter. I freely admit that in those early days, I was often a little afraid that these type of explosive confrontations would end in a fistfight. But they never did, and as I grew to learn more of the Balkan temperament, I understood more. The other two drivers were Petar, who was tall and dark-haired, and Mikhail shorter and stocky. Ilija whispered that they both thought that they should be driving the hire car, but Franjo had told them in no uncertain terms that it was his honour, not theirs. Informing them, with an air of superiority that, he could speak English, and they couldn't put an end to the discussion. I could barely understand a word Franjo said, both then and later. But I never let on and always tried to adopt a knowing expression and an air of fully understanding everything he said in English. However, the essence of what he wanted to tell me he was always able to communicate and we spent good times together. He was a man of wisdom and incredible kindness and whom I deeply respected.

We were heading for an area in the North East of Yugoslavia called Baranja. It is almost heart-shaped and lies between the Rivers Drava and the Danube, with Hungary bordering it to the North, Croatia to the West and South and Serbia to the East. In ancient times, it had been part of the land mass that had been under the Pannonian Sea and as a consequence is a fertile farming area and is also very flat. Baranja is part of an area known as Krajina, meaning the lands at the edge or border of the realm. It was also a buffer zone. In the 17th Century, the Serbian people fled North with the Austro-Hungarian army before the invading Ottomans. They were allowed to live in Krajina by Leopold II, the father of the Austro-Hungarian Empress Maria Theresa, as both a reward and bribe. Although Serbs had lived here before this time, he needed many more of them to populate and continue to defend the area against the Ottoman Empire. The Ottomans or Turks had invaded and occupied parts of Hungary, Serbia, Bosnia, Bulgaria, Greece, Romania, Macedonia and present day Albania.The defensive, Serbian settlements of Krajina stretched all the way from Hungary in the East, across parts of Bosnia and Dalmatia to the Adriatic coast. This entire region was part of the Austro-Hungarian empire right up to the end of the First World War when in 1918, under the Treaty of Versailles it became the Kingdom of Serbs, Slovenes, Croatians. However, the new kingdom also now included, Bosnia and Herzegovina, Kosovo, Macedonia and Montenegro, all ruled by the Serbian King Aleksander 1st Karageorgeovic. In 1929, he renamed the Kingdom Yugoslavia, meaning Southern Slavs.

Our journey was finally over when, some 5 hours later, we arrived in the village of Cheminac, across the River Drava, about half an hour drive from Osijek. Bumping and bouncing along a rutted track we finally reached Franjo's farmhouse. Ilija was beaming broadly and could barely contain his excitement as our car drew to a halt. He had been abroad for the past seven years, and this was his first visit home in all that time. There was another exceedingly, warm welcome from the family and friends awaiting our arrival. Maria, Ilija's step-sister, was not at all like him. She was dark haired and black-eyed, a little shorter than me and belied her 38 years. For, although she was as round as can be, with red cheeks and twinkling eyes, she only looked like a young girl. Now all the introductions were made. Ilija's mother, Baba (grandmother) Vida was a tiny, frail little person. She solemnly embraced me, kissing me three times on the cheek which I was to learn was the Serbian way of greeting. Others kissed only twice, this being the Catholic, Croatian tradition. I eventually developed a 'seventh' sense which was to pause for a fraction of a second, after the second kiss.Then, see if the person I was greeting, was moving in for a third kiss or beginning to turn away.

Franjo had no other relatives, apart from his nephews, living in Baranja for after the death of his father, his mother had gone to live near Zagreb with one of her daughters. His four brothers had

of somewhat muted, celebrations. I remember seeing a New Year tree and oak branch behind closed doors in the family sitting room, with no outward sign of any festivities to casual visitors. Ilija's sister is Serbian Orthodox and so Christmas Day falls on January 7th and New Year's Day on January 14th, the difference in dates is due to the two churches using different calendars. The Julian Celestial calendar, introduced by Julius Caesar in 45. B.C. is that employed by the Orthodox religions. The Gregorian calendar was adopted by the Catholic and Protestant churches in 1573 at the order of Pope Gregory. He sought a solution to the problem that the Julian calendar was inaccurate in celestial time, and the solstices and equinoxes did not coincide with it.

I experienced a twinge of regret to see that traditional Christmas trees played no role in Christmas celebrations. It was set up on New Year's Eve and then discarded before the eldest male member of the family cut an oak branch in the forest and carried it into his home on the 6th January. On Christmas morning, he cut a piece of wood from this branch and stoked the fire with it and as the burning wood sparked and crackled he made his wishes before the gathered family. Declaring may there be as many children in this house as there are sparks in this fire! Or, may there be plentiful livestock and crops this year!

Interestingly, this tradition seems similar to that of the Yule log and almost certainly also dates from pagan times. The largest oak tree near a dwelling place was venerated, by pagan Serbs, as a temple of Perun, the most powerful of their pagan Gods. And still today the oldest oak trees, in rural areas, are considered holy, as a tree of the Covenant and are blessed by the Orthodox priests. The local people bring offerings of food and drink to lay under the branches, especially in times of drought or other hardship. On some days, an open-air mass may be held, the tree a focal point with lighted candles set under its branches.

The Orthodox Christmas is a very simple and beautiful celebration, without all the trappings and gifts that I was used to. A little basket of straw is on the floor, underneath the family's table or, a scattering of straw lays over the floor and guests cast sweets or some coins into it when they arrive. Later the children are allowed to search in the straw for these treasures. A huge, circular loaf of bread is baked for the most important holy days. An intricate pattern of plaited braids is laid around and on top of the loaf. In the richest families, a gold coin was hidden in this bread, in the poorer ones, silver. Nowadays, any gifts the children receive, are usually given as New Year gifts.

However, there are some similarities between all these festivals of whatever faith, and that is the endless supply of food and drink served from morning until late in the evening. I thoroughly enjoyed this time and far from feeling like a stranger was now happily joining in with the day's chores and afterwards relaxing with this most friendly of families.

Ilija suggested we explore the area and meet some of his childhood friends who lived in and around Cheminac and in his mother's village of Ugljish. I was going to be introduced and was full of dread. Despite his reassurances, I was acutely aware of the fact that I am twelve winters senior to him. While Ilija told me my fears were unfounded and that this would be of no concern to anyone else, I was nervous. Especially so because an old friend of mine in the UK consistently referred to him as 'your young fella'. I felt like an old harridan with an Adonis in tow.

We visited about three houses a day over the next four or five days. We travelled to perhaps five or six local villages to the homes of Ilija's friends. Some of the unwed sisters of Ilija's friends eyed me with a certain amount of hostility, and I assumed from this, shall we say, that they had probably been very close friends of Ilija. Well, after all, it had been seven years since he had left. Plenty of time, to heal a wounded heart one would think. Ilija for his part was surprised at this perception of mine, but then men do not have that naturally occurring intuitive feminine radar with which we are equipped!

I had asked Ilija to teach me a few words of Serbo/Croat so that I could, at least, exchange the usual courtesies with my new friends. I learned that 'molim' meant please and that 'hvala' meant thank you. Or so I thought. Ilija also taught me the full form of 'would you care for some coffee?' or, zelite li nesto da popijete? This sentence is a very formal way of asking if someone would like something to drink. In my entire time here, no one has ever said it to me. It is typically shortened to, 'hocete kafu ili nesto drugo? Meaning would you like coffee or something else? I listened attentively for the formal phrase but didn't hear it. Happily, I recognized the word kafu, and so I replied 'molim' to this less formal enquiry about a drink. I was confident that they had just asked me if I would like a coffee and I had replied, 'please.' The question was repeated. 'Hocete kafu?' and I again smiled and said, 'molim.' The question was now put to Ilija and coffee followed very quickly. I waited until we left and were in the car to ask Ilija why they hadn't understood me when I had said 'molim.' 'Oh, he replied airily, 'molim has several meanings. It can mean, thank you are most welcome or, thank you or, it can also mean, please repeat what you just said I didn't hear you.' I groaned, so they thought I was deaf! The usual reply is 'moze' which means alright. Not very satisfactory in English etiquette but, adding hvala or thank you to 'moze' seemed to be the best solution. I advised Ilija never to answer my Mother or other English friends with an 'alright,' as a form of polite reply!

On these early visits, I again ran into trouble with customs related to food! I lay the blame for this squarely at my Mother's door. A typically English attitude to their children is that whatever they take to eat, they must finish, not even a crumb to be left on their plate. This was particularly true if, someone partook of a piece of my Mother's cake. Some unfortunate girlfriends or, boyfriends of mine or, my brothers, were forever condemned by Mother for leaving something half-eaten. The unspoken accusation was 'why don't you like my cake?' Now, as we made these visits for me to meet Ilija's numerous friends and their families, out came the cakes, coffee, and wine. As a well-drilled daughter, I knew how to behave as a guest and ate the first slice. When this was promptly followed by a second, I manfully struggled to finish that too but, rather shamefaced, left it half eaten.

After about an hour, we left amid hugs and promises to return soon to visit more friends in Knezevi Vinogradi. Again we received a warm welcome and more cakes, wine, and coffee. I could have refused, but that would have seemed churlish, so I asked Ilija to ask them for a small piece of cake. I did indeed get a smaller slice and since these cakes are delicious had no problem eating it all. Another slice quickly appeared on my plate. 'I don't want any more' I hissed to Ilija, and his reply was; 'well for goodness sake, leave a little; by eating it all they think you are still hungry.' This observance of what I perceived as good manners, along with pouring soup over our dinner. And drinking tea all day, despite the fact that you are not ill, is on a long list of things that Ilija (and most people who live in this area) view as specifically English eccentricities. Indeed, according to Ilija we, the English are genetically eccentric. This pronouncement came after I had explained the rules of cricket to him. Especially about leaving the field for lunch and tea-time. And he gave several other reasons such as; to appear always to carry an umbrella even in summertime. Even after 27 years together he becomes exasperated with my insistence on the form; will you please and not, you will. They even have a saying 'Sta se pravis Englez?' which in essence means 'why are you doing it the English way when there is such a simple solution.' Meaning, why are you making such a fuss about an ordinary task?

However, there is much affection for the English among many people. One elderly man, we visited in 1991 shook my hand vigorously and told me that he still had a jumper, part of a consignment of clothing, parachuted as aid from an English plane in 1946! He had been a soldier in King Petar's guard during the First World War and showed me a faded photograph of himself in uniform in pride of place on the wall. The couple were old family friends, of shogur's family and Ilija knew I would enjoy meeting these two very sweet people. He was 88, tall and silver-haired and still carried himself very proudly. He cared for his tiny little wife who was 86; she was bent and nearly blind. They were very traditional and lived in a small house with very narrow doorways that you could only pass through by turning sideways. I assume that this style of the traditional doorway would have afforded the occupants some defence against the invading enemies of those past times. As we entered the inner room, he took my hand and led me into another smaller room. Where hanging on the wall, there was an enormous photograph of the late Serbian King Aleksander 1st.

'How is our new dear King?' asked this dear old man. 'Could you get me a photograph of him please I don't have one?' He knew that the claimant to the Serbian throne lived in London. And he made this request when Ilija told him of my admiration for Prince Tomislav, brother of the late King Petar, who I had been working with on the Serbian Lobby. That most excellent of men and his wife worked tirelessly for Serbian people in need, I had no contact, nor did I seek any, with Aleksander, Prince Tomislav's nephew who declared himself as Crown Prince of Serbia. Now they insisted that we stay for coffee and tenderly, the old man helped his wife to prepare it. It was as though we had stepped back in time. They both wore traditional, embroidered clothes and everything about the room was simple, with beautifully crafted chairs, a wooden table covered with an embroidered cloth. I dreaded putting my coffee cup anywhere near it and so I held it until I had drunk the coffee and then put it in the sink. Ilija did too, for he was as equally moved as I, by the sight and actions of these two dear people.

One of our visits was to a very remote farmhouse and was the last of the day. I had consumed numerous cups of coffee, glasses of wine and assorted cakes during earlier visits that day. And so now I asked to use their bathroom, and Ilija asked his friend's mother to show kindly me the way, and she beckoned me to follow her. It was not the first time I had used an outdoor privy but, what followed was positively a first for me. She led me to their barn, opened the door and indicated that I should go inside. It was their cowshed, and I searched for a privy. She poked her head around the door and pointed to the floor, smiled a little and left. 'Needs must' I thought to myself and pulled down my panties and squatted. Then the cow, who had been eyeing me and who I had thought tethered, began to advance towards

19

me. I was squatting and with weird shuffling movements, made it to the door. I vowed to kill Ilija when I next saw him. Returning to the farmhouse, I tried hard to appear quite nonchalant and completely unruffled and used to all 'that sort of thing'. Trying hard not to give them the impression I was some snobby foreigner.

I need not have worried Maria rounded on him when we got back to Cheminac, and he told her where we had been. 'What on earth were you thinking? What will she think of us?' She scolded. As Ilija related this conversation to me afterwards, he looked at me very seriously and said told me that if I were serious about coming to live in Yugoslavia, then life would be different. Probably very strange and hard to get used to for a while. If I couldn't adjust and accept the changes, I would never be happy. It was a valid point; I was out of my comfort zone. However, I took the opportunity of warning him that when my Mother and Jude came to visit, as they surely would, he had better make sure of more modern facilities than those!!!

Could I adapt? It is arguable that while the English make a laudable show, on the surface at least, of being welcoming and solicitous to unexpected guests, in practise it can be non-existent. How many times in the UK have you arrived, unannounced, at a friend's house as they are about to eat? What is the most likely outcome? Retreat in embarrassment and confusion? Be shown into another room and supplied with a drink and an apology? Or, as they do here, would they pull up another chair lay another place and everyone enjoy their meal together? If I choose to live in a different society then, it is not they that must adapt, but me. I would not offend any society I lived in by being deliberately offensive to their individual customs, religions or beliefs. However, we are our Mother's children and have been so well-drilled in some things that are almost impossible to change.

These were early days; I had still not yet made a decision, as to whether I would become a permanent resident. I had made enough financial investments to allow me to live a moderately comfortable life without working and which would give me the time to seriously consider my future. I was not about to jump into a second marriage yet. But, we did go house hunting in the nearby town of Osijek. We had begun to make plans for our future. I loved the relaxed pace of life here. I had often thought that when making new acquaintances in England, the question about your job would often be secondary to how much you earned. Here they seemed to be genuinely interested in you and had far more leisure time. Academic success is admired and applauded as are the many cultural, historical and art societies which receive much enthusiastic support. In fact, it felt as if I had stepped back in time, to the period in Coventry as I was growing up. We could play our children's games in the streets because there were few cars to be seen in those days. Television programmes were limited. Only the pangs of hunger or the fall of dusk drove us homewards. I hadn't wanted to commit myself to any permanent commitment up to that point. It had been barely six months since the end of my marriage. But now, as I looked around, I knew that if the relationship between us could grow and thrive then I could very likely be happy in a place such as this.

CHAPTER THREE

We found a lovely little house in Osijek and negotiated a rent to buy agreement with the Hrastnic family who lived nearby. Their matriarch was something of a tyrant. With peroxide blonde hair swept up into a top knot, she waddled her way into my life each day showing me that she meant business. If I failed to clean the driveway of our house in the morning, she would arrive with her broom and do it. Then she came with more cleaning materials and motioned to the windows. Although irritated, I allowed the sweeping, but nothing more and consoled myself by addressing her as Gospoda Hrastnici. Hrastnici is an Albanian name and Ilija had told me that the family had recently changed their name from this to Hrastnic, being in their view a more acceptable Croatian variation. The first time I called her Gospoda (Mrs) Hrastnici was accidental, but, when she rushed to me and said 'Ne! Hrastnich! Nije (not), Hrastnichi!' When I saw how much irritation was caused by my mistake then, of course, she forever became Gospoda Hrastnichi. And she came less often

My first, lone, trip to the local piazza or marketplace and the nearby supermarket was quite memorable. I had been driven by a sort of desperation because Ilija had told me that the only thing they used in Yugoslavia to make cakes rise was yeast. Untrue! Flour is sold without a raising agent unlike in England where it integral, but they do sell baking powder in little sachets, that is if you know what it is! I knew very few Serbo/Croat words but was undaunted by my first lone, shopping trip. At the local supermarket, an exceptionally friendly shop assistant had encouraged me to smell different types of food to try and identify what it was. She solved my problem with the baking powder and quite a few other things over the months and years to come. However, another, not so helpful assistant always refused to sell bread to me if I used the Serbian word hleb instead of the Croatian word kruh. These differences were regional differences within one Serbo/Croat language but, gradually Croatia had sought to introduce many new words trying to differentiate and create two different languages. Fortunately, Croatian academics poured scorn on this idea, and although differences remain, they are slight. I did try to use the most acceptable form but some words like kruh I found hard to pronounce because of the harsh guttural sound needed.

I relished the idea of visiting the local piazza and unhesitatingly, using my limited language to buy salad, I enquired of a stallholder 'Jedan salata molim?' (May I have one lettuce, please?) He began to fill a carrier bag with the lots of lettuce. Apparently, people here didn't buy just one, so he assumed I meant a kilogram. Despite this poor start, gaining confidence, I recklessly pointed towards tomatoes, gherkins, and other fruit and vegetables but, to my relief he handed me the carrier bags, and I just took as much as I wanted. I still had the kilo of lettuce, but pride didn't allow me to admit my mistake, and I bought all of them, there seemed to be about 12! I was pleasantly surprised by how cheap everything was and began to make my way home loaded down my purchases, four bags in each hand, now regretting I had walked and not driven here. I had only gone a very short way when 8 or 9 youths approached me. They stood in front of me and avoiding eye contact; I tried to move past them. They were laughing and chattering, and I felt hands taking the bags from me. Thank goodness my handbag was hung across my chest that at least was safe, and I hurried towards our home which was only around 500 metres away. Ilija was standing at the gate and as I ran towards him. Reaching him, I gasped, 'They stole my shopping and they are following me'. 'No' He laughingly replied 'They are our neighbour's boys, and they just wanted to help you with your bags.' And I turned to see them just behind me. 'Tell them I need the bathroom or something!' I hissed at him, not wanting them to realise what I had thought. I needn't have worried; they had already guessed, and Ilija and they were all laughing at what they thought was a huge joke. Ilija was on excellent terms with all our local teenagers. They regularly swapped comic books, and he often helped them with their school homework. From that day whenever I went shopping, if they were around, I never had to carry my shopping home from the local shops and piazza.

In the former Yugoslavia and now in Serbia and no doubt the other new, neighbouring republics, drunkenness, especially in public, is neither admired nor part of society. Especially not amongst young men, and certainly not the girls. In the entire 27 years that I have travelled in and around the country, I have never seen the type of public drunkenness that is sadly so apparent in the U.K, especially at weekends. With scenes, there of young men and women, helplessly drunk, lying outside clubs or pubs or fighting each other that are rarely if ever seen here. Balmy evenings, spent in the pavement cafés, hold no fear of being spoilt by the exploits of drunken bores. It was also a very safe place for women and children. One December afternoon I was visiting Rada and although it was only four p.m. it was getting dark. She had a 7-year-old daughter, in her first term at school and now due home and I offered to go and meet her from school because she was preparing their evening meal. She looked surprised and said 'No, she will be quite alright but, thank you.' I asked if she had any concerns at all. She said 'Why would I worry? She knows the way home, it's not far, and she doesn't have to cross any busy streets.' She had no conception of her child being in danger from strangers. Children go to school from the age of seven and usually walk to and from their school alone (if they do not have to cross busy streets.)

Early one evening I met up with a couple of girlfriends and we set off to walk to one of their homes, dusk was falling, and it was gloomy with very dim street lighting. I began to look around and after a couple of times, they asked me if I was worried about getting lost. I was glancing around to see if anyone was following us but hesitated to say so because they really would not have understood my concerns.

I knew perfectly well that rapes, sexual assaults and other acts of violence were not widely reported in the newspapers and certainly not sensationalised. But, amongst the people I knew in Osijek and Baranja, few seemed to know of or ever discussed any such crimes. It was a welcome realization to someone coming from England that women and children could go out alone without any fear of being attacked or worse. Both adults and children frequently accepted lifts from people they barely knew. And I felt totally uninhibited about chatting to children I didn't know, either on the street or, while shopping. In the 1950's and 1960's when I was growing up, we had enjoyed the same freedom as these children. Although I once encountered a 'flasher' when I was around 12 years old and my girlfriend and me, giggling like mad, ran to our homes, and I calmly joined the family at tea. I ate some sandwiches and then in a lull in the conversation I announced rather grandly 'Daddy, a man outside opened his trousers and showed me his 'winkle.' My father, choking on a mouthful of food, jumped up roaring and ran immediately down the hallway to the front door where he saw a policewoman standing, she had been alerted by my friend's family. There followed an acutely embarrassing interview which, for me, was far worse than the flasher. Winkle was the only word for what I saw that they could winkle out of me. Then it was over, and I was forever instructed to 'run all the way home' whenever I went out.

I was so impressed by the security of this new and wonderful place of mine that I wrote a letter to one of the English national newspapers. It even appeared in the Osijek local, daily newspaper called Glas Slavonija. In it, I offered Yugoslavia as an alternative retirement destination to Spain or, France. As a result, we got about twenty letters from British pensioners asking about house prices or if there was a National Health Service in Yugoslavia. Some were from people saying they were too afraid to leave their homes for fear of being mugged. A very sad reflection I thought on British society in the late 1980's and early 1990's. It also reflected the social climate of that time in Yugoslavia where there was no indication, on the surface at least, that war was coming. It was truly a lovely place to be.

I was still travelling back and forth to the U.K, the Netherlands and Germany and several times, work permitting, Ilija came too and in England, he met all my nearest and dearest. Ilija's acceptance of everyone, whatever their religion or race, was never more apparent than when we were staying at my parents' home in Coventry. He answered the door to two Jehovah Witness representatives and soon showed them into one of the sitting rooms. Appearing in the kitchen, he told my mother that he had two guests, and she immediately offered to make them all tea or coffee. Ilija returned to his guests, and my father took them the tray of drinks. When he reappeared, his face registered a look of disbelief. 'They are Jehovah Witnesses!' he said 'I always tell them, no thank you, not today and Ilija invited them here! We will never get rid of them now!' I tried to reassure him that Ilija would explain to them that he was the only one interested in having any discussions with them. That he was just interested in what they had to say and enjoyed debating different opinions regarding the Bible. My father told the story for years, even though the Witnesses never returned.

However, it was not to be my last meeting with Jehovah Witnesses for they came several times to our house in Osijek. On one visit, when I was suffering severe back pain, one of them manipulated my lower back as I lay on the dining room table, and I remember wondering what my dad would say! They were friendly people and Ilija enjoyed his debates with them, and I wonder at the commonly held view that they should be summarily cold-shouldered. I was now making lots of new friends; Ilija was re-connecting with his old ones, and we were enjoying life. I can honestly say; no one mentioned their ethnicity. Not our friends, nor Ilija and so I repeat, the shock of the civil war between such friends, when it came, was all the more.

The horror was still to come and before it did two people, in particular, became very close friends. Mitzy and her husband Paul had returned to spend their retirement in Osijek having spent much of their working lives in America. Paul was Hungarian and had been born in a concentration camp during the 2nd World War before emigrating to the U.S.A as a young man. His wife Mitzy was Croatian and had been a displaced person after the same war, living in a chardak (small wooden storage hut) with her family until they too had emigrated to America in 1949. They told us how they had dreamed of spending their retirement in Yugoslavia and had just bought themselves a little house in Osijek. They lived in the next street to us with a large, friendly Doberman dog who had also accompanied them on their journey from the U.S.A. It was Mitzy who taught me to make bread and some favourite specialities of Ilija like poppy seed cake, all kinds of strudel and goulash. She was a professional cook, and as soon as you entered her house you always caught the aroma of something delicious wafting through from her kitchen. They were later to have to return to America, their dream of retirement in ruins, but for now, they could live their dream.

I was travelling to England every six weeks or so because my father was unwell and I still had to deal with my divorce. We were busily setting up an agency. Several companies, both in the UK and in Yugoslavia, had approached Ilija and me with proposals for us to represent them and to arrange visits from those UK companies interested in forming trade links in Yugoslavia. We set up a bank account with Slavonska bank in Osijek, and I soon discovered what a very unusual approach to their clients this bank had!

We stood at one of the open counters, having waited patiently in line in one of the very long queues always evident whatever day we went. The bank teller, unsmiling and rather tersely, asked me to open my pass book. Because I hesitated and she was about to shout at me, Ilija intervened and told her I was English. At this, others in the queue started leaning over my shoulder looking at the pass book. I wasn't exactly happy about this but decided, for now, to be quiet. Then, Ilija passed over our latest, monthly telephone bill which was to be paid by giro from this bank. The cashier took one look and said 'Odakle vam toliki racun?' She turned to a fellow teller showing her the bill and both of them exclaimed loudly 'Boze! I knew this meant 'Oh my God.' Ilija, whispering, told me that they were amazed by the size of the bill. They had asked him who we had been calling, 'It's nothing to do with them' I replied, 'what a cheek!' Then, the queue

27

got involved too and had a general discussion on who we must have telephoned and how long we must have talked. Addressing what seemed everyone in the vicinity Ilija now answered them all in Serbo/ Croat. 'She is an English lady living here, and her father is ill and so apart from visiting him every couple of months, she likes to call her Mum most days to see how they are.' Applause broke out, smiles and handshakes. At the time, I had no idea what Ilija had said, but I smiled and accepted the adulation.

Balkan banks still have their own and very individual charm, including the conditions of use of the credit cards they issue. You may use their card only after depositing enough money as a credit balance on the card before you can spend an amount equal to the credit. And in our local bank in Valjevo if you wish to withdraw more than a few hundred euros then you must place your order and then wait until they open the safe. What time do you open the vault questions, are met with a smile and a shrug. And if the information is forthcoming, it is, that the time varies every day, so, come back in a couple of hours or so or, possibly tomorrow, more smiles. Like it or lump it, that's the way it works! In one matter, they do not differ from any other bank in the World. You can always have a bank loan after first proving to the bank that you don't need one. We planned to build a house in Jagodnjak, across the river in Baranja but it was difficult to save, with all the costs of my travel and paying for the current house.

Now we began to advise one the companies, called Auto Slavonia and helped them plan a programme of sales, merchandising and staff training. When the first containers of car accessories arrived from the UK, included in the delivery were some promotional prizes for the sales staff. There were audio equipment, radios, and a T.V. prizes for the salesperson achieving the best month's audio sales figures. The store manager was horrified at the idea because he thought it would naturally be his. He was wrong.

On another occasion, a group of UK buyers came to visit the local Belje food production factory. This state-owned company was a large and important supplier of all forms of fresh and processed foods to the region. In addition to the visiting buyers there was the Belje management team, and so, Ilija found himself trying to translate for 15 individuals. Finally, everyone sat down to lunch in the director's dining room. While making the arrangements for this meeting, Ilija had tried to explain to the representatives of Belje the differences between Balkan and English business lunches. And probably, that the famed Balkan tradition of making endless toasts with rakija (plum brandy) resulting in a certain level of drunkenness would be unwise on this occasion. After an excellent lunch, everyone was enjoying their coffee and small glasses of plum brandy or whiskey. Ilija suddenly stood up and walked over to a large, plush couch. He apologized in both Serbian and English saying that he needed to have a nap and lying down he promptly fell asleep.

I thought that to pretend that this was the most normal behaviour in the World was most appropriate. The Yugoslavian hosts assumed this was yet another strange English habit while our English guests smiled at yet another little Balkan foible. Looking rather bemused, our party of 15 spent the next half an hour or so drinking lots of coffee while trying to understand each other. We did surprisingly well, not least because most Yugoslavians, learnt a second language and often a third language at school. Some had learned English and although, not fluent; it was possible to communicate quite well with them. Ilija finally awoke refreshed, and we resumed our tour. I have since successfully used a similar subterfuge on occasions when I have made a dish or cake that has not turned out well and announced almost apologetically that, 'that's the way English people like it.' It works very well.

Most of the visiting companies were very impressed with what they saw, others not so. We had been approached by the local government regarding a small castle, outside the town of Valpovo, about 25 km North of Osijek. In 1945, it had been confiscated from a Hungarian family and was currently used as a museum, and now the local authority sought investors to renovate it. Perhaps to convert it into a hotel or conference centre. It was to be a joint venture with the local government retaining the majority share. We arranged for a visit and were met by the members of the local municipality. It was evident that a sizeable investment would be required because the castle was quite dilapidated but, the building itself was very impressive and at first glance, quite sound. As we climbed some stairs to one of the large reception rooms, our castle guide pointed out an enormous crack that ran from the top to the bottom of the stairs. Asking Ilija to translate, he said. 'You see, this castle was stable until the earthquake struck and caused all this damage, but, of course, it can all be fixed.' We tried valiantly to put a positive spin on it all but never saw the investor again.

I always looked forward to the weekends which, whenever possible, we would spend with Ilija's family in their village which was about a half hour drive from Osijek. Crossing the bridge over the river Drava, just outside the City limits and with little traffic on the road. It was a pleasant drive across the flat landscape, past the endless rows of corn which seemed to stretch endlessly into the distance. Near Cheminac, where there was a beautiful old oak forest we would have to drive cautiously because roe deer would often emerge from the trees, leaping across the road in front of us. Their intention was to ravage the new shoots of the season's corn or graze on other crops, much to the fury of the landowners.

Sometimes we saw spectacular lightning forks shooting all around us to the distant horizon some 10 to 12 km away. Most people worked on Saturdays and so it was on Sunday that family gatherings took place. Occasionally, Maria and Franjo took some of their holiday entitlement when they had important farm work to do, such as harvest time or when the pigs were slaughtered in the autumn. It was usual for neighbouring farms to help each other and family too and so for these jobs there were, usually, at least, twenty people working and consequently, twenty or more mouths to feed. I usually offered to wash up and tried to keep out of the way of the women rushing about. Apart from the sweetcorn harvest, when I helped the women strip the leaves from the cobs of corn which the young men then packed into the chardak, the little purpose built houses used to store sweetcorn. I learned to enjoy a little nip of plum brandy if it were cold especially with a cup of the intensely sweet and strong coffee made here. The art of making and the drinking of it is almost ritualistic. Ground by hand in small brass coffee mills, it is then added to the little open coffee pot in which water has been brought to a boil and then set aside. After stirring the coffee into the hot water, it is quickly brought back to a boil and like unwatched boiling milk will soon spill its contents all over the hob if not carefully tended!

I was slowly learning the language but still not enough to be able to chat freely with everyone. However, we managed to understand each other and most of the children were learning English and tried to help. Sometimes a misunderstanding could have hilarious consequences. One such was when I asked my friend, Rada, in Osijek, to buy me four packets of greaseproof paper for the cakes I was baking for our approaching slava (the family saint's day). I asked her for kolaz paper (collage paper) and received four packets in assorted colours. Looking at her rather quizzically, but not wishing to offend her, I asked if it could withstand high temperatures. This conversation went backwards and forwards until she finally realized that I didn't want to produce works of art, but to bake cakes. She began to laugh and told me that what I really needed was kolach or, greaseproof paper.

The slava is quite an event and not a task taken on lightly. When I unsuspectingly agreed to take on the responsibility of holding it, after Ilija's mother Vida had 'passed it' to him, I was in for a shock. The family saint is St George, a happy coincidence since he is the Patron saint of English folk. There are many saints' days celebrated in Serbia, and each family has their main slava, passed down through the male line of the family. Then there are others such as the mother's slava and sometimes several other smaller, saint's days to celebrate. Here is a strong link between Christianity, tradition and paganism. There must be no work done on these holy days, except for the housewife who works from dawn to dusk, cooking and serving the guests. She is indeed fortunate if she has family members to help her because most guests will not. Their role is to come and enjoy the food, singing, and dancing and, of course, repay such hospitality when they hold their celebration. Whether Ilija thought I could rustle up an army of fairies to help me, I have no idea. But as I blithely launched into the planning and preparation I slipped into the management role of days gone by and asked certain pertinent questions. How many people would come? What time would we have lunch? I had yet to attend a slava and so I assumed it would be rather like a Christmas day! I think the term is a happy idiot. The answer to how many people was around sixty or so. And it would begin around midday and probably continue until around nine or ten in the evening.

I think my mouth was still open when he added that we would probably have to feed the band too. One of the 'by the ways' was that the family will usually descend on you around midday. Probably friends and others, having called in on lots of other slavas on the way, will arrive in the evening. The next day, those unable to make it on the first day would come. I baked twelve large cakes and got totally carried away. There were cakes of every colour and flavour. Large pink fondant, dark brown chocolate, yellow banana flavoured, orange layered and white vanilla a quite stunning array! The only meat served is either a sheep or suckling pig which is roasted the day before, either by a friendly baker or, by the men of the family. It is a great social event for them, a happy all-male time, when they can sit around a fire all day, drinking beer, turning the spit, gossiping and totally guilt free. The preparation of the meat is their sole, responsibility and naturally, nobody criticizes them for doing nothing else. Meanwhile, the ladies prepare an enormous saucepan of sarma or stuffed cabbage rolls and finally, the all-important soup. No cheating with packet soups either. The meat and vegetable have to be produced, served with a tomato sauce dip, as they had on the evening of our arrival in Cheminac. Koljivo is a special dish of cooked wheat prepared with walnuts and sugar. This special dish is offered to each guest before they begin their meal accompanied by a sip from a glass of red wine; it is almost like taking communion as people cross themselves as they accept this offering.

When I asked Ilija about the origins of this tradition, I received the answer I always get to such questions. Not only from Ilija but everyone else I ever asked which is, 'hmm, no one knows, it comes from a very long time ago.' But he added the following explanation about Easter eggs, which I found interesting. At Easter, in every Christian, Balkan home, hard-boiled eggs are beautifully decorated by mothers and their children. Guests are invited to select one these eggs, and they will try to crack their egg against someone else's without breaking their shell. I assumed that this tradition was Christian. However, Ilija told me that ancient Babylonians offered decorated eggs to the Goddess of abundance and rebirth, Istar or Astarta. And thus the tradition pre-dated Christianity by around 4,000 years!

The guests usually arrive as a family unit, and there is a continuous procession of people drinking coffee before they eat or, taking Koljivo, on their soup or meat course or, enjoying the cakes. When one of our slavas, was being celebrated later in Beli Manastir, the day was terrifically hot; we laid out all the tables in the garden. Within minutes of proudly placing the cakes on the tables, they began to melt, fondant and cream gradually sliding down the sides of the cakes! The weather is no more predictable in Baranja than in Britain! We have celebrated our May slava in the snow, torrential rain and brilliant sunshine!

There are certain rules of the Orthodox Church that cover this family slava. On the morning of the celebration a huge, freshly baked, round and beautifully decorated loaf of bread is taken to the church to be blessed by the priest. And following the arrival of their kumove, the male kum and the (male) head of the family ceremoniously break the bread. The hostess makes sure that each guest is served a small portion of this special bread. If the date coincides with a time of fastings, such as before Christmas or Easter, then everything is prepared without any dairy or meat products and fish is eaten. Although valiant attempts are made to produce 'post' or fatless, eggless cakes, they are normally awful!! Only oil is permitted in the preparation of food at this time. In some areas of Serbia, two days of every week are set aside for fasting days and before Christmas and Easter, fasting can last for up to 7 or 8 weeks. Many people still observe these periods which some explain enables them to enter a state of deeper contemplation and reflection. There are few obese people in Serbia and perhaps fasting is a contributory factor, however, what I have seen are, some rather fat priests?

I have rarely seen such generosity towards one's guests as I witnessed at these gatherings. Everyone is constantly plied with food and drink. The host and immediate family hover over the proceeding with a genuine eagerness to ensure that each person is thoroughly enjoying themselves. They rarely join in the feasting; because they are too busy tending to new arrivals, those at the table or those taking their leave. I tried several times, as a guest, to offer my services with the tea towel but was firmly shown back to my seat. That is not the way; I was told but also warmly thanked for the kind thought. I secretly thought there was something malicious in the way some of the women delighted in being waited on by the lady of the house who often looked, and almost certainly was, exhausted. However, they wore an aura of exhaustion as a badge of honour, inexplicable to outsiders like me!

In later years, after we had moved to Serbia and yet another home, Vida asked the local priest to come and bless it. She was very devout but rarely tried to influence others, however in this she was implacable. She would not live in a house that had not been blessed by a priest. We awaited the visit and fortunately for us the day he came, Vida was out visiting a friend of hers. The priest, newly graduated, started a theological discussion with Ilija. I was to him introduced as Amanda the English alien and with a flick of the wrist, he dismissed me. They were talking about fasting, and I couldn't follow all the arguments. The priest turned to me and said triumphantly 'so you English don't fast?' He had annoyed me now. 'No' I replied. 'But,' I replied, 'I often wonder what you do with all the food you don't eat for the fasting period, do you give it to the poor?' Ilija shot me a warning look because if the priest reported back to Vida that we had insulted him, we would be in trouble. 'I have a freezer' he replied. He stood up and began to bless the house, and as he turned his back to me, I realized, to my horror, that he had been sitting in a chair recently vacated by one of the cats. His immaculate, black robe covered with cat hairs all over the area of his backside. I didn't feel that I could go up and brush it off without offending him, and so I did nothing and said nothing. What a coward! Ilija led the way out, and they parted at the gate. I asked Ilija if he had noticed anything about the priest's robe and he replied 'Oh you mean how new it looks, it probably is.' I was so glad Ilija hadn't seen the hairs; he would not have kept quiet.

During the time we lived in Osijek on a visit to Vida, at her farm, she had asked me when I was going to see my parents again. After telling her the date, she said that she was going to prepare a roast suckling pig for me to take to them. I told her somewhat regretfully because my parents would have loved it that I couldn't take it with me. Looking at me with some astonishment, she asked me how many kilograms I could carry with me on the plane. Finally, with further reassurances that it would fit into my case, she added. 'What if you told them it was from your kum?' (Which once again underscored the importance in society of one's kum). I valiantly tried to explain that H.M. Customs would not allow me to import it into the U.K. She thought for a moment and then asked me how they would know I had it if I didn't tell them what was in my suitcase? I explained that they searched people's luggage sometimes. Undeterred, she asked me why anyone would search people's luggage. Desperate now, I told her that some people might try to secrete snakes or a dangerous animal in their baggage to take into the country. 'Oh!' She said triumphantly. 'Certainly because they hope they will bite those horrible customs men!'

I hadn't the courage for explanations regarding the fact that most English people would fail to understand the importance of one's kum. For explaining what the Church of England meant had been testing enough; sympathy is probably the best way to describe her reaction.

CHAPTER FOUR

Many of my friends in the UK, asked me the following question. 'So what is it all about then?' When I talked of the civil war of the early 1990's. Their questions were probably out of politeness more than interest. If your eyes, as theirs, begin close as I answer, then I apologise.

The cause is complex and so, I suppose, will be the remedy. Perhaps a South African-style truth and reconciliation campaign could have been more successful than Nuremberg-style revenge. One thing is sure I still hear these words. 'Never forget, Never forgive, Never again' Serbians said them after the end of the second World War, hoping fervently that the acts of ethnic cleansing would never again occur. So what *were* the historical tensions and what *was* the troubled history of the Balkan peninsula? What had allowed those, with their agenda, which was to manipulate the population into what was to become a vicious and vengeful civil war?

This gateway to the Orient has been fought over for centuries, and the first, recorded invasion of the Balkans was by the Roman Emperor Trajan in around A.D.91. Finally, following the decline of the Roman Empire around the 5th Century, the Kingdom of Serbia emerged and covered an area similar to that of the Former Republic of Yugoslavia. However, in 1389, after the battle of Kosovo the Ottoman army defeated the Serbians and despite numerous uprisings and attempts to liberate and restore the Serbian Kingdom up until 1865 the area was under Ottoman rule. During this lengthy occupation some Serbs and other Slavs, in Bosnia in particular, had converted to Islam either by force or for convenience or had just converted.

The three main religions in Yugoslavia were Catholicism mainly in Slovenia and Croatia and increasingly in Kosovo with the massive influx of Albanians who had fled there from a harsh dictatorship in Albania. Islam, in areas of Bosnia and also amongst some of the Albanians in Kosovo and parts of Macedonia and Raska in Southern Serbia. And, Serbian Orthodox in Montenegro, Eastern Croatia, North and Central Bosnia, Kosovo, Eastern Macedonia and throughout Serbia, with other minority religions such as Calvinists, Jews, Jehovah Witness and others. Quite a patchwork!

The Serbs continued to live in Baranja along with ethnic Germans, Hungarians and small Croatian, Roma and Jewish communities. Evidence of this is found in the number of predominately Serbian Orthodox and German or Hungarian Calvinist Churches and also the cemeteries from that period before the 2nd World War. Under the Treaty of Versailles in 1918 following the defeat of Germany, its allies, and the Austro-Hungarian Empire, Baranja became part of the Kingdom of Serbs, Croats, and Slovenes. King Aleksander 1st of Serbia changed the name of his Kingdom to that of Yugoslavia (southern Slavs). In 1932, The King was murdered in Marseille by a group of Croatian extremists. The late King's brother Prince Paul became regent because the new king, Peter 1st, was still a minor. Serbia had lost over 52% of its male population of fighting age, fighting on the side of the British and their allies in the 1st World War. They now tried desperately, as the 2nd World War loomed, to remain neutral. However, in 1941, Prince Paul went to see Hitler and sought to appease him by agreeing to demands allowing Axis forces to march through the Serbian Kingdom, to attack Greece was their objective. Their real target were the oil fields of the East. On his return from Berlin in March 1941, the Regent was overthrown by Serbian Army officers and other prominent Serbs.

Early in the morning of the 6th of April 1941, a furious Hitler sent his Stuka bombers to attack Belgrade, decimating the city and his troops immediately invaded the Kingdom. Ante Pavelic, the leader of the Croatian, political, fascist party (Ustashe), returned from exile in Mussolini's Italy. On his arrival in Zagreb, he immediately declared the Independent State of Croatia and allied himself to the Third Reich and its allies, declaring war on Great Britain and their allies. Croatia did not occupy Baranja, which was seized by another Axis ally, Hungary along with Vojvodina while Hitler's army occupied the remainder of Serbia.

During the 2nd World War Pavelic's Ustashe government, established concentration camps, the two most notorious being the Jasenovac and Kerestinec camps, near the Croatian capital of Zagreb. They were extermination centres where men, women, and children of Serbian, Roma or, Jewish ethnicity, who had been living in Croatia, along with dissident Croatians killed with great savagery and barbarism. Even today the real number of those murdered is unknown but was thought to number in the tens of thousands. German sources reported at that time that by July 1942, Croatia was reporting that not one, single Roma was alive and living in the land. Some Serbs, dissident Croats, Jews and Roma managed to escape into Baranja then occupied by Hungary. The Hungarians did not have any policies regarding the extermination of these groups in this area, unlike their actions in Northern Serbia where they committed widespread atrocities. Croatia also occupied a Northern part of Serbia called Srem. In 1942, the Nazi concentration camp, called Sajmishste, on an island in the River Danube, was handed over to the control of the Croatian Ustashe. Many thousands of Jews, Serbs, and Roma, men, women and children, gathered from all around Serbia were sent to their deaths their deaths there.

After Victory in Europe over the Axis forces in 1945, a victorious Marshall Joseph Broz 'Tito' declared his intention to create a new, Socialist Federal Republic of Yugoslavia. The president of the Soviet Union, Josip Stalin, was confident that he could maintain total control over the New Yugoslavian Republic. At the Yalta conference spheres of influence within the European states was agreed between U.S.A, Britain and U.S.S.R. The fate of millions of people living in Eastern Europe was decided, without their knowledge or consent.

Although there were still some close ties between Tito and Stalin, by 1948 Stalin had denounced Tito. Branding him, a traitor of the Great Communist Idea, he called upon all loyal communist officers of the Yugoslavian Army to depose him. But, it was Tito who retained power, and it was not until after the death of Stalin that good relations were finally restored between the two countries.

Much of the new Yugoslavia lay in ruins. The Serbian capital of Belgrade had been reduced to rubble, first by German Stuka in 1941 and ironically, by the allies in 1944 when over a thousand civilians were killed and just 18 Germans. The leader of the Yugoslavian Partisans, later to become President of Yugoslavia, Josip Broz 'Tito', was responsible for the brutal repercussions enacted against the royalist Chetnik forces with mass executions. Those ethnic Germans, who had not fled with the retreating Axis forces were executed, imprisoned in labour camps or brutally expelled and forced to return to Germany. This despite most of them having lived in Baranja for generations and many died on the journey. The Jewish population had disappeared into the Croatian and German death camps along with many of the Roma and as a consequence many farms and villages in Baranja were now empty, its owners gone, never to return. The new communist government offered all citizens of the new Yugoslavia, from Bosnia, Croatia or Serbia the opportunity to repopulate Baranja and move into some of the deserted farms and villages, which many thousands did.

These events between the years 1945 and the early 1950's namely the seizing and redistribution of land and assets by the new state were to have a profound influence on the attitudes of those populations. While the majority of the churches were left intact, what was once the Jewish Synagogue in central. Osijek seems to have been incorporated and used by adjacent businesses including a bank. When, at the beginning of the civil war in 1991, families were forced to leave their homes in Croatia or Baranja there was certain ambivalence by those unaffected by the moves. Many had lived through the previous upheavals or had learnt of it from parents and grandparents. It is difficult for an outsider to comprehend this mentality unless they have experienced the turmoil of those war years. Under the umbrella of being a citizen of Yugoslavia, ethnic Serbs, Croats, Roma, Hungarians and others living Baranja had continued to celebrate their differences of religion, languages and ethnicity. There had been considerable intermarriage which was to have tragic results for many of such families.

Under the Communist land reforms, each citizen was entitled to 15 acres of land. Large tracts of land and private estates were nationalized and handed over to state enterprises as collective farms, and one of these in Baranja was Belje. The former property of the Esterhazy family, who were related to the Habsburg Dynasty, it had covered vast acres of land stretching from Hungary to the Danube in Baranja. Now it became a thriving enterprise and a principal employer for the area and food production for the Federation.

In the summertime, their workers tended fields of sweetcorn, sugar beet, tobacco, corn, yellow rapeseed and tall sunflowers, turning their giant heads to face the sun. Fields of delicate poppies stretched as far as the eye could see. Interspersed with smaller fields of bright yellow, green or red paprika, tomatoes, and gherkins. Later came the melons, squash, and giant pumpkins. The orchards of plum, cherry, apple, quince, pear, medlar scattered across the land, and there were vineyards, climbing the gentle undulations of the terrain. It was an incredibly picturesque landscape of vivid yellow, green, red, blue and green hues. Each little farm had their acres of land where they grew their crops and raised their livestock. Some of their produce and livestock, they sold, under contract, to the Belje Company or at the local piazza. Most people had a day job too, working for the company in either their factories, shops or cultivating their land. Ilija's mother was one of those that raised pigs and sold them to Belje as did Franjo and indeed many other farmers in the area. Many also had their day jobs working for this or other companies. Those seeking employment usually had no problem, although there was a definite climate of jobs for the boys, or, not what you knew but who. The mood seemed to be of general satisfaction with their standard of living, the free education for their children and free health care and security of employment. They could expect to retire at the age of 55 with a guaranteed pension.

However, this was a Communist society. There was no freedom of speech and those, including some priests of the Serbian Orthodox Church, who tried to oppose Communism had, in the past, paid the ultimate price or, imprisoned. In 1945, Tito had taken on the enormous task of rebuilding a federation that had been decimated by war. The Croatian part that had allied itself with Hitler and its Ustashe government had murdered hundreds of thousands of Serbs, Roma, Jews and political dissenters. The Catholic church in Croatian had been party to the killings and forced conversions to Catholicism of Orthodox Serbs. Mile Budak had been Minister for Religious Affairs for the Ustashe Croatian government 1941-45. He had stated that their goal was the conversion of one-third of Orthodox Serbs to Catholicism, one-third to be exiled and one-third to be exterminated.

There had been a vicious, Serbian, internal struggle between the royalist Chetniks and the communist Titoists Tito had to take on the reunification of what were arguably seven different countries, Slovenia, Croatia, Bosnia and Herzegovina, Macedonia, Montenegro, and Serbia. In 1943, Tito, quite arbitrarily, presided over the redrawing of all their borders. Borders were redrawn without proper consultation, representations, legal or historical justification and moreover, with tragic consequences, an utter disregard for ethnicity.

This decision inevitably to led to the civil war. The large Serbian populations living outside of Serbia in the Croatian communes had been largely untroubled or were even unaware of these new borders or thought them irrelevant because they were part of Yugoslavia. Then there came the dramatic break-up, which was a complete shock to many of its citizens. Suddenly they were being asked to declare themselves as a citizen of Serbia or Croatia. In effect, they were stateless because most had to apply for citizenship in either newly independent country. Most importantly Baranja had never, ever been a part of a Croatia; a Croatia that had been a mere duchy or province of the Habsburg Austrian Empire since the end of the 14th Century up until Hitler helped his ally establish a state in 1941.

For this reason, the Krajina Serbs either sought to live in a separate enclave or to become part of Serbia. Or another alternative many fervently wished for, the return of an integrated Yugoslavian state once more, where ethnicity had not been such an issue for them. There either had to be a mass migration of ethnic groups again or, they had to fight. And that decision was, to all intents, removed from their hands as political debate escalated into violence.

Beneath the apparent success story of a new Yugoslavia risen, phoenix- like from the ashes of WW2, lay a deep distrust and almost palpable fear of Croatian Nationalism, by the ethnic Serbian communities of Croatia. These concerns, however, were not manifested until after the June 1990 election of Franjo Tudjman. He set in motion the plans for his party's new, authoritarian, ultra-right-wing policy of Croatia for Croatians and published his articles expounding his theory that Jews had run the Jasenovac concentration camp. And the people looked on in growing disbelief.

However, this was 1988, and the citizens of Yugoslavia seemed to be content with their lot although, as with most people, hoped for a little more. Many of the state-run industries offered their workers some excellent benefits, for instance, Franjo could use his company's caravan and campsite on the Adriatic for a small nominal fee. There were free spa centres where some workers had a right to receive free treatment. By law, every company had to provide apartments for their employees. After fifteen years of continuous employment, ownership passed to these employees. If there were no available flats or as an option, employees could obtain loans at extremely low, interest rates to build their homes. University degree courses were free, and there were places for all those who met the required standards. Many employers would pay monthly stipends to the children of their employees, which did not have to be repaid if the students achieved a degree.

The list of benefits, laid down by the state, for employees, was quite incredible. There was a real emphasis and financial support for adult further education too. I was amazed at the number of compulsory subjects the children studied at the state schools; fifteen was the norm and up to 25 if they were specializing in math at gymnasium (sixth-form) level. All students from the age of around 12 years studied a second and often a third language, usually English, Russian or French. I soon learned to dread the look on the faces of the children when we visited some families. I would be introduced as 'the English lady' followed by 'Now, speak to her in English, come, show here how much you have learnt'. Poor children! They would avoid me like the plague after that. Parents here are incredibly supportive of their schools and teachers. Even today, despite little prospects of finding a job following the economic collapse, parents struggle to send their children to university for, nowadays, it is not free.

There were only two events which made me acutely aware of the fact that this was a Communist State. The first was when one of my new girlfriends Rada arranged to meet me and take me to an aerobics class in Osijek for I was very keen to stay fit. When I arrived at her flat in Osijek, there was another friend of hers, Rosa, waiting to meet me and eager to join us for the aerobics class. As we strolled along Rada was talking about the Partisan Centre where we were taking our class. 'Do you know what a Partisan is Amanda?' She asked me. 'Yes, it is someone who fights for their country against invaders I suppose, like a Cetnik or Partisans or others like them,' I replied.

But, as I said these words she suddenly stopped walking and horrified she turned to me saying, 'hush! You must never say that! Of course, it doesn't mean that! It means only the people who fought with Tito!' Rosa glared at me and without a word said something to Rada and walked off. Rada looked genuinely upset as I vainly tried to explain the English language definition of Partisan does not restrict it in that way. Rada was quite agitated telling me that Rosa was the daughter of a high-ranking Communist Party official who might well report what I had just said to the police. I thought she was behaving far too dramatically but the evening was spoilt, and I returned home. I told Ilija what had happened and to my amazement he too was concerned. 'You have got to be so much more careful of what you say; you won't be held accountable. But, they may well assume I told you to say that, and I they will arrest me!' In the event, we heard no more, and I became more guarded when expressing opinions. I also made a point of avoiding Rada's girlfriend after that night; she would never be a friend of mine. I long ago accepted that some people think I am an arrogant, probably wealthy stranger who thinks she is much better than anyone else. I have through the years tried to prove them wrong but, as in all societies some prejudices are too difficult to overcome.

The second event was when Ilija received a summons for an interview at the police station in Osijek and questioned about his time abroad. They wanted to know where he had been and what he had been doing. He seemed to accept this procedure without too much concern, but I didn't, and it went on the minus side of the plus and minus box of my plans for my future.

I had never thought about the freedom afforded me by living in a democracy and was used to questioning, criticising or praising decisions made on my behalf by an elected British government. I like the fact that no single member of Parliament is protected or assured of re-election.

Now, imagine if you can that society has fallen apart. Shattered by two world wars as it was in Yugoslavia and then a charismatic leader emerges from the throng, offering redemption. He presides over economic recovery and the rebuilding of devastated towns and cities. Unemployment rates are negligible, the rights of the citizens and workers extremely well protected by exceptionally good terms of employment and holiday pay. Which includes the right to a year's paid maternity leave, two years if you had twins! An excellent health service is free. As is an education system which virtually guarantees free university places, with only minimal charges for accommodation and food. And there is a remarkable law that states the theft of books isn't a crime, and so there is no prosecution! There are equal rights for all and for probably the first time Roma people do not experience any form of discrimination. There are many other social benefits for everyone too numerous to detail, and the result is that people are, in the main, satisfied with their lot. People are free to worship in the way they choose, except for pacifists such as Jehovah Witnesses who face imprisonment if they refuse to serve in the army. Every male has to serve a fifteen- month obligatory period of national service in the armed forces, delayed until after graduating from University on application. There are no official religious holidays, however, but people find a way to circumvent this obstacle with unofficial days off. Because their religious calendars differ, Serbians worked while the Croatians celebrated their Holy days and vice-versa. The downside is no freedom of speech or freedom to travel abroad without meeting certain conditions. A somewhat simplistic view but, how the average person seemed to regard the state in the latter part of the 1980's.

The cult of having influential friends able to manipulate the system laid the seeds of corruption, which germinated following the demise of this charismatic leader and father figure called Tito. The ambitions of the leaders in each federal state were now to lead to the downfall of what Tito had hoped would be a legacy of a United Yugoslavia.

Around this time, I was invited to join the annual outing of the local women's group and was astonished to witness them sobbing, visibly distressed as we filed past Tito's tomb in Belgrade. There seemed to be a genuine affection for his memory amongst them. These women were a mix of ethnic Croats, Serbs, Hungarians and Roma. I didn't know for sure who was what because no one was counting in 1988.

I also had my first run-in with the law in 1988. I was driving through the town of Vukovar. We were on our way to the airport in Belgrade to catch a flight home to England. Our usual habit was for me to drive there and Ilija would drive home. Now I must admit that I was knowingly breaking the law. Yugoslavian policemen had always been unfailingly kind and courteous to me and so despite a stern warning from Ilija, I never took my driving licence with me. Why? Because I was afraid of losing it and had reasoned that if I lost my passport, then, at least, I had some form of identity.

A traffic policeman wearing his white cap, white belt and sleeve covers stepped out from behind his vehicle and waved me down. I stopped the car and realising full well he was going to ask me for my driving licence I put all the papers inside my passport and smilingly handed them to him. Returning my smile and with a charming salute, he took the passport and papers and looked through them. 'Madame' He said 'Molim vas, vasu vozacka dozvola!' I thought excellent! He doesn't speak English and now tried telling him I was English and didn't understand what he wanted. Before he could reply, a voice piped up from behind me and in Serbo/Croat Ilija told him that I knew perfectly well what he was asking me. That I always refused to carry my driving licence, just because I didn't have to in England. I had completely ignored his repeated requests to do so here and so the policeman should please punish me with a fine to teach me a lesson. Now the officer took the role of devil's advocate. 'Oh, but she is a guest, she doesn't realize what the law is here' said he to Ilija. Ilija was quite furious by now and said 'She does know our laws, but she just will not listen to me!' 'Very well,' said the officer. 'Madam, I must punish you! 2 dinars for, not carrying your licence, please remember next time,' Ilija said 'No, that is not enough!! She must pay at least 5 dinar! And write her a ticket!' 'Oh, no' said this lovely man, 'that would be too harsh, no ticket and 2 dinar please' I paid him the equivalent of 10p and drove off. From then on I carried my licence unless of course I forgot!

CHAPTER FIVE

The Summer of 1988 was sweltering, and Ilija and his friend Georgie made plans for us to go and spend some time on the Adriatic coast. We would provide a car, and they would provide the accommodation. Ilija was very vague about both the destination and the accommodation, but I was untroubled, a sort of a happy idiot state of mind, entirely unaware at this point of time of the Balkan psyche. I knew that it was to be an overnight journey to avoid the unbearable daytime heat and would last approximately 12 hours. I prepared very carefully with night-driving glasses, iced flannels, extra socks, a little neck pillow a cardigan and a blanket. We had also packed all kinds of boil sweets, fruit, drinks, and sandwiches. Our friends had a little daughter who sat in the back in between her mother Jasmina and I. We gaily set off around ten p.m. Two and a half hours late, but who cared! We were off on holiday!

After about an hour, Georgie realised that he had forgotten his driving glasses so could he borrow mine, please? An hour later their little daughter was getting fractious and wanted to lie down to sleep. My pillow and blanket helped achieved this. Jasmina was cold, time for cardigan and socks. I knew the time for flannels had arrived after we had all had some chocolate and Georgy wanted to wipe the steering wheel off because it was sticky. I sat frozen, blinded by the passing headlights while all but the driver and I slept. We stopped around dawn and pooled all the food for an early morning picnic. The sun was rising, and I was feeling a bit brighter for there was an end in sight. About four hours later we began to pass row, upon row, of caravans. Ilija had 'sort of' suggested that we were going to stay in a small villa. As we passed them, I shuddered and told him that I had never understood why anyone would want to holiday like this, especially with children. There was absolutely no comment from anyone. We pulled up outside the tiniest caravan I have ever seen in my life. Ilija sprang out of the car, not daring to look in my direction and grandly announced that we had arrived, and he was off for a swim. He shot off and didn't return for a couple of hours, having judged that by then I would be in a more reasonable mood.

I did try my best, but with communal showers, primitive toilets and sharing a single bunk with Ilija, in that tiny caravan, was a holiday to forget! I will not go into detail about primitive toilets which required one to squat. Enough to say that I ended up constipated for the whole ten days. Aged 19, with student friends and without access to any facilities on a camping holiday that saw us travelling through France and Spain down to Marrakech in North African, we had solved our problem. We had just walked unhesitantly into the grandest hotel in sight, cheekily using their bathroom facilities! Had it not been for meeting lots of really nice people, great barbeques, brilliant blue sea and endlessly sunny days I probably would have given Ilija a very rough passage. It was fun, and it taught me a very, valuable lesson regarding any occasions when Ilija is vague about arrangements.

One of Ilija's closest friends, Joseph and his wife Jelena, called on us in the autumn of 1989 inviting us to the marriage celebrations of their eldest son, Mario. I was thrilled because this was to be my first, Yugoslavian-style and, after all, who doesn't love a good wedding? I immediately rang my dearest friend, Jude, to invite her and was delighted when she said she would come from Coventry in the UK. We had been close friends for over 20 years and possessed of a truly indomitable spirit; she has never hesitated to be by my side should I need her support or, her mine. As long as she is not required to enter a lift or sleep in the cabin of a ship below deck, without a porthole, then she is up for anything.

Judith Winters, with the marvellous maiden name of Loxley, is a quintessentially English lady, from her perfectly coiffured head to her tiny size 3 feet, her perfectly manicured nails, matching shoes and handbags are legendary. And a steadfast refusal to accept anything other than 5-star service from even the most humble of establishments makes her appear a lot taller than her diminutive 4ft 11inches as she confronts the miscreants. Jude spent many years working within the probationary service and never once was troubled by any of the criminals under her watchful eye. After some discussion, it was decided that she would wear a beautiful crepe de chine, black-spotted white dress, and a saucy little, white fascinator. I was to wear my favourite colour red, also crepe de chine and also a fascinator, mine was red and adorned with large red poppies

It was a gloriously sunny day, Jude and I stood, a little self-consciously, with the rest of those gathered outside Joseph's house. We saw that the weddings here were much more informal than those in the UK. We were the only ones wearing hats; everyone else much more informally dressed but, we were soon surrounded by a friendly crowd of these friends and family, everyone happily chattering and hugging each other. The musicians arrived, and I was a little disappointed to see that it wasn't the usual Roma group. With their double bass, usually with one string, trumpets, drums, and violins, they created their own distinctive and very vibrant music. Instead, it was a more sober group of friends with their guitars. I was to learn later that this was a nod to local sensibilities for, despite some tensions; each family was going out of their way to make the occasion neutral. Tensions? But, I wasn't aware of any tensions.

This area had been subjected to major upheavals during its history. Following the resettlement of the mostly abandoned village began in 1946, after the ethnic, German families fled before the advancing Red Army, Joseph's village, Cheminac, was resettled by mainly Catholic Croatians. Whereas, the bride's village of Ugljes had a Serbian, Orthodox majority who had settled there in around 1661 after receiving a charter from the Habsburg emperor, Leopold 2nd. Many of the ethnic Germans who had settled in Baranja had done so, after fleeing the Plague, in Southern Germany in the late 16thC. In 1729, the Habsburg rulers of the region even erected a monument in the old town of Osijek, which locals call, the plague monument. Although the area was affected by the disease, it had not been as devasting as in other parts of the empire. Tradition has it that they built the monument as a talisman in the hope that it would keep the town free from future outbreaks

Simmering below the surface of this seemingly united state of Yugoslavia was a fervent desire for independence by some Croatians. Fuelled by a resentment and hatred of what many regarded as Serbian oppression, it was to erupt like a tinder-dry, pine forest on a warm balmy evening. Whether this yearning, by the Croatian nationalist, was understood, was certainly not evident to an onlooker such as me. Josip and his family were staunch supporters of Yugoslavia, and Josip probably realised his marriage as a Croatian to a Serbian wife could be affected by such changes. However, I do not believe that even he dreamt that it would ruin his life and destroy his family.

Roma bands usually provided the music at Serbian festivals and weddings as they were to at mine and Ilija's. But, they did not play at Croatian events because there was still an uneasy relationship between the two ethnic groups after the genocide of the Roma in Croatia during the 2nd World War. Now the music and singing began as Josephs's son; Mario emerged from his father's house with his Kum, Ivan (best man) and Kuma (wife, fiancée or partner) in close attendance. The bridegroom's party, in their specially decorated car, headed the procession of cars. To further stress his importance, the Kum and Kuma wear special sashes, traditionally sewn and embroidered by the groom's mother while he is still a baby, ready for this most important day. We were heading for the home of the bride Liljana, in Ugljes, a village about four km away. With horns blaring and flags flying, we drove along until the cars suddenly all stopped outside a neighbour's house where they awaited the bridal with trays of drinks. After partaking and toasting everyone and everything, we all drove off again. There was a beautiful arch above the gateway leading to the bride's home, garlanded with fresh flowers, and a large group of friends and neighbours were gathered to welcome everyone. Mario's kum approached the door of the house and Lilijana's father, Milan appeared in the doorway with a stern expression on his face. Now Mario's kum Ivan began to negotiate the price of the bride, a tradition that is nowadays more lighthearted than serious. He offered a dish which Milan gruffly refused, then television, which again was brushed aside until, finally a fitted kitchen was suggested, which, feigning reluctance, Milan accepted and then led the way to a very tall pole with an apple speared to the top. Mario was handed a rifle and everyone waited, some with baited breath, to see if the prospective groom could prove his fitness to be a husband. Which had to demonstrate by a shooting prowess in shooting the apple from the top of the pole. He took careful aim, shot; the apple exploded everyone embraced and amid wild cheering and applause his bride-to-be, Liljana, emerged shyly from her parent's house.

A beautiful girl, with long brown hair that was swept up into a chignon and a circlet of fresh flowers, held her short white veil in place. She wore a high waisted, ankle-length, white lace dress which had short capped sleeves and a modest neckline. The men began firing their hunting rifles into the air, and the women whooped with joy as Mario, grinning from ear to ear, stepped forward and stooping, shyly handed her a bouquet of white and pink roses. I glanced at Jude, who, despite having a finger in each ear, was smiling broadly and thoroughly enjoying it all.

The wedding party now moved into the garden where tables were laden with food, a huge variety of fresh and smoked meat and sausages, pickles, preserves and great loaves of fresh bread. The toasting began again and continued until we were ushered into the cars once again for the return to the groom's house, the bride and groom each travelling separately in their kum's cars, which led the procession. With headlights blazing, car horns blaring, flags flying from the open windows of the cars or the radio antennas and cheered on by other cars and onlookers, it was an exhilarating journey. On our return to Mario's parent's home, the older members of his family were waiting outside to greet their new daughter. Everyone hugged and kissed and then we all formed into another procession led by a flag bearer. Now came the group of musicians and then the groom Mario, walking between his kum and kuma. Next, the bride with her kum and kuma and behind them family and friends. The parents and grandparents of the couple do not join the procession. Instead, they all stay at the house of the groom or at the place of the reception, to greet the guests when they come from the wedding. Their task is to oversee all the preparations for the feasting, which is either held at the groom's home or in a local hall or restaurant. Jude and I were both surprised to see that the parents of the pair are absent and that it is the kum and kuma who have the most prominent role at a wedding.

There was not going to be a church wedding, for both families were communists and so about 20 of us squeezed into the local registrar's office. The couple made their solemn vows to the registrar, to the strains of the waltz from Tchaikovsky's The Sleeping Beauty. In fact, the music was so loud, that it is hard to hear all the words. It didn't seem to bother the participants at all who just raised their voices.

Spilling out of the small office we in the wedding party were now met with more music, gunfire, clapping and embraces as a huge crowd of well-wishers gathered to escort us to the village hall. There the spacious room quickly filled with happy and excited people of all ages and as waiters served welcoming drinks, their kum made their speeches, and we all toasted the couple. Then the band struck up and almost immediately everyone began to dance. It's a traditional dance where everyone holds hands, single file as they dance around the room, up and down the aisles, passing between the tables with others joining in as they passed by. A bit like the hokey-cokey but with a bit more decorum!

Jude and I sat at one of the long tables, in our hats, wondering when they would serve the food. A couple of hours later, we still sat waiting, but not alone as everyone came over to meet and greet us. We helped ourselves from the bottles of soft drinks, wine, beer, whiskey, brandy and mineral water stacked on each table, and still wondered about the toasts and food. Suddenly we were swept up by some of the dancers and joined a long line of them which was still snaking around the room. Jude put a brave face on it and tried to learn the steps but looked a little bemused and probably deafened by the loud, insistent thumping of the music. With much relief, we saw the soup arriving because by now it was about three p.m. and our day had begun at around six a.m. in Osijek.

Ilija found us and led us back to our table where we now, abandoning our hats and even our shoes, enjoyed a magnificent wedding feast. Course after course came, but at the same pace as usual and so it was around six p.m. before they cleared the tables and the cakes appeared. Every friend of the bride or family makes and brings cakes to the reception. I had made two large chocolate gateaux, and so had most women; there was certainly an abundance of them! All different shapes and colours, ranging from enormous gateaus to very dainty squares and slices, each had been lovingly decorated by the women and were delicious. There was a traditional wedding cake which was cut by the happy couple, and everyone tasted it. Coffee followed the champagne and we all were wondrously full! Suddenly, the man sitting next to Jude jumped up picked up his glass and dashed it to the floor shouting 'Ziveli!' Meaning long life! Jude turned to me and gasped, 'did you see what that man just did, what a hooligan, I didn't think they had hooligans here I *am* surprised!' With that, another stood up and dashed his glass to the floor and then another and another, including Ilija. Jude was speechless. Ilija rushed to her side and explained that this was called 'crashing the glasses' and it showed how happy everyone was, and didn't she think the weddings here fantastic! Not like the way the English hold theirs, which in his opinion were more like funerals. Jude said 'Yes, but why break these glasses? They look ok, not old or anything?'

And now I saw that Jude was biting her lips. 'Hey, don't worry, they are just celebrating' I said as I put my arm around her shoulder to give her a reassuring hug. 'I would hate to see them when they are miserable then.' She said and then, grumbling a little, 'how can we dance now with all that glass everywhere?' I motioned to Ilija, who grinned and went off to find a dustpan and brush. Then he cleared up the mess around us, and all was calm again, calm again that is until the guests discovered more unspent ammunition and began firing outside the Community Hall. Judy was also unnerved by this, and it was evident that she could not connect gunfire to a celebration as everyone else at the party did. 'Besides which,' she enquired of Ilija, 'where do all those bullets go that they fire into the air?' He did not answer her, and I was to ask the same question of him a couple of years later! The celebrations continued and then at around 10 p.m the 'Brides Dance' began. The bride now had to dance with every single guest in the room and have her photograph taken with each of them. In return, the guest put money into a large bowl, held by her kum seated close to the dance floor. The more flamboyant of the guests flung hundred mark bills into the bowl. Others, less so, demurely handed over a white envelope and those that had a small contribution, furtively pushed their hands inside to drop in their gift. This gift can often be the only present for the couple from some friends or family. However, sometimes they receive a traditional gift for their home and, also, some cash. The amount collected can often be a substantial sum and is intended to help the young couple finance a new home or even a car. Jude and I both took our turns to dance a few steps with Liljana. We stayed just long enough to watch the groom on the stroke of midnight, as he swept up his bride into his arms, and to great applause, carried her out of the hall to their home. As soon as they left, we made our tired but happy way home too.

Holiday Honeymoons are unknown here. The newlyweds will usually have just a few days alone before they rejoin the family and resume their daily work and chores and it is usual to live with the groom's family. Eventually around retirement age, the groom's parents move into a smaller house that they have prepared in the grounds of their home. The elder son and his wife take over the larger dwelling. It seems to work very well, however as in all societies, I did meet some vindictive mother-in-laws. Nevertheless, most brides seem to be able to find a way to make their lives happy. No doubt the mother-in-law, at some point, realizes that their daughter-in-law is going to be the person to care for them in their old age. For unless the old person has no living relatives, it is almost unheard of for anyone to enter an old people's home. Our friend Joseph owned a Café, which his wife ran, and Liljana seemed happy to help Jelena. Often the family would have a company apartment in the nearby town, and because all the secondary schools are usually in the cities, the schoolchildren would use them during the week and return home for weekends.

Next morning I returned to take up my usual position and help with all the washing up. Much of it had been done by volunteers the night before, but they had left us the huge catering trays which had held the roast lamb and pork. I had left Jude at home in our spare bed with a note telling her to help herself to breakfast and we wouldn't be too long. She would have immediately volunteered to help, but with her immaculately painted talon-like fingernails I really couldn't inflict any more shocks on her, because there wasn't a pair of rubber gloves in sight! It was not her first visit to see us. She and my mother had come six months earlier, and we had spent a wonderful two weeks at Easter with them. Our Mother liked to check where her chicks were. One of the places we took them to see was a historic tavern in Baranja. Here according to legend, the Austrian Count Esterhazy lost his fortune to a gypsy girl. She so entranced him with her dancing that he threw more and more gold coins at her so that she would dance. For several days, he kept the tavern locked with only the dancer and the Roma band inside. He sent his servant back to his castle for more and more gold. Finally, telling him to fetch all the gold that he possessed and threw this too at her feet. When the servant reported that there was no more gold, he realized he was ruined. And so he sent his servant one last time, to bring him his gun with which he shot himself. There are many legends concerning the vagaries of the Esterhazy dynasty and their links to the Habsburg's of Vienna.

Dear, kind Franjo took several of his precious, holiday entitlement to show them around too. He took us all to see one of Tito's hunting lodges, a small palace called Tikves. And on another day, we all set off for Djakovo about 70 km South-West of Osijek to visit the

Lipizzaner stud. These world-famous horses were originally bred in the nearby village of Manduchevac, by the soldiers of the Austro-Hungarian Habsburg rulers, to supply these beautiful horses to the Austrian Court in Vienna. Ilija and I had been before in our capacity as agents, for the stud farm was also seeking investors interested in expanding the company.

On another trip, Franjo took us all to Batina; a tremendous battle was fought here in November 1944 between the Red Army and their allies Tito's Partisan forces against the retreating German and Ustashe armies. It lasted for nearly a month, and there were heavy casualties on both sides. There is an imposing monument set on a hill overlooking the River Danube below and beneath this monument, there is a mass grave holding some 1300 Russian dead. Batina is at the edge of the territory of Baranja marking the border with Serbia. The bridge is one of only two crossing the Rivers Drava and the Danube, into Baranja, the other bridge being the one to Osijek. The views from the monument are spectacular as Batina dominates the surrounding area. It is not difficult to understand why so many died attempting to ford the river, to scale the heights, to attack the German positions. The River Danube ran red for many days during the carnage. It was a significant battle and led directly to the fall of Budapest in Hungary because it gave the Red Army a substantial bridgehead on the West bank of the River Danube.

It was a moving experience, especially for my mother who had survived the destruction by German bombers of her hometown of Coventry, in the U.K, in 1941. After the worst raids, heavily pregnant, she was evacuated to the village of Lubenham, near where my father was working at a factory building the Spitfire fighter planes.

Franjo now had a treat in store to lighten our mood a little. What happened next was one of the highlights of their holiday with us! Firstly, they were able to see the storks nesting on top of the chimneys of some of the houses in Batina, and another precariously perched on top of a telegraph pole. The nests, made of reeds and grasses, measured several feet in diameter, and many garlanded with some peculiar objects that the birds had gathered to integrate into their nest. These included a pair of black stockings waving in the breeze, plastic shopping bags and other strange pieces of cloth. Franjo explained how the birds liked to nest in occupied buildings, not empty ones. He told the story of the local school that had a pair of storks who had returned each year to their nest for several years. Which, by the way, all the surviving storks do every year with their same mate, to the same chimney, to the same nest. This pair of birds arrived to discover that the school was now empty because a new one had been built about a mile away. They immediately abandoned their old nest and quickly made a new nest on top of the new school! Some residents cover their chimney pots in such a manner that the birds cannot nest on their houses. But, many others do not because they believe that it brings great fortune if the birds to choose to share your home with you! These are the white stork variety; the rare black storks only seem to nest in Kopachski Rit, a nearby national park.

Now, he took us to meet some of his Hungarian friends in the community and after sharing the customary offering of strudel and coffee we all walked up the steep hill to the top of the village. All along the right-hand side of the road are little wooden doors behind which are natural caves or others that people had cut into the sheer walls of the cliff face.

Opening up the doors to one of these caves our host invited us inside where there were huge vats lined up along the walls. Here, the local growers of grapes produced and stored their wines. Excellent Rieslings, rosé, red wines there were sweet and dry to taste including Cabernet, Traminac, and Sauvignon amongst others. Some they sold themselves at the market or to passing trade, or, if tested and approved by their chemists, Belje Company would buy it and sell it under their labels. There were, at least, a hundred of these caves located in the almost exclusively, ethnically, Hungarian village of Batina. The residents of Batina were prolific wine producers and the going rate for a litre of wine in those days, if you took your bottle, was about 12p a litre for a most excellent wine. Our Hungarian hosts showed us all how to taste the wine, and it flowed freely. However, because of a certain hesitancy on my mother's part to spit it out, we soon became aware that she was beginning to become a bit unsteady on her legs. Franjo once again took charge and whisked us all off to lunch. We found ourselves at a restaurant on the edge of the Kopachski Rit National Park. We enjoyed a late lunch of goulash with noodles, made from wild boar and deer meat, cooked over an open fire in a kotlich, or cauldron in the same manner as fish soup. And it was served with hunks of homemade bread and a fresh, shredded, white cabbage salad. We had a table outside, and I think it was an unforgettable experience for all of us, sadly never to be repeated with all of us together again.

More opportunities for fascinating journeys of discovery now presented themselves to Ilija and me through our work with our agency. We were invited to explore Kopachski Rit, a vast area of wetland forest between the Rivers Danube and the Drava. This wilderness was for centuries a hunting ground for the nobles and later the country's President Joseph Broz Tito. Later still, came the wealthy tourists who travelled to Baranja and paid for the opportunity to hunt stags and wild boar. With an area of over 23,000 acres, its very inaccessibility protected its wildlife inhabitants from man. We were extremely fortunate for unlike today, no jeeps or other intrusive motor vehicles were allowed into the national park.

We had to travel by rowing boat or by horse-drawn carriage. The latter form of transport afforded us a unique opportunity to see wildlife completely at ease with the sound of hooves, unlike the sound and smell of a motor vehicle. Accompanying us was a dear friend, who was also a resident biologist at the reserve and a guide.

Beginning our journey just before dawn, we slowly drove through the forest and had our first view of tiny, yellow and brown striped, wild piglets, noisily chasing their mother. Not very long after this the driver slowly brought our little carriage to a halt and motioning us to be quiet and still, pointed towards an area of very tall grass. I could see nothing and then quite suddenly a large animal appeared in a clearing ahead of us. At first, I thought it was a fox but as soon as I used my binoculars I could see it was a large cat. My very first sighting of a wild cat! I could only marvel at its lithe, thick-set body;

it seemed to move in leaps, alert to the slightest sound or movement. And then it was gone as quickly as it had appeared and our guide told us that in all his time working on the reserve he had only ever had two sightings of the wildcat. We felt very privileged indeed!

There seemed to be thousands of birds swooping and diving above us, for this was spring, and there were migratory birds, returning to claim their nesting sites. Wild geese, ducks and huge flocks of cormorants, heron, both white and the very rare black storks, swallows, swifts and egrets to name just a few of around 291 species to be found there. As the carriage made its way slowly through the trees, we saw the shadowy forms of red and roe deer moving in what seemed to be big groups. A solitary, wild boar, with large tusks, head and rump in the air and seemingly unaware of intruders, trotted along the track ahead of us.

Now we approached an open area with a large, but somewhat squat, solitary oak tree almost at its centre. As we drew closer, Chedo, our guide, told us that we were about to see a nest of a white-tailed eagle. They had not yet returned to lay their eggs, and so we were allowed to go much closer than usual. We saw an enormous nest. It seemed to stretch the entire width of the tree, and the depth was around 2 metres or so. I was surprised to see how low in the tree it was, compared to an Eagle's eerie! Once the birds returned to breed no one was allowed to come anywhere near the area for fear of disturbing the birds. To be in this wilderness of largely unexplored forest was remarkable and we both felt hugely privileged.

Later in the day, after boarding a small boat we visited one of the lakes, within the reserve. Here we saw a huge colony of nesting cormorants and water snakes, as they swam alongside our little craft completely unafraid of us. Finally, he guided our small boat on what proved to be an utterly incredible journey. We followed a small water course which briefly brought us out into a fast flowing River Danube!

It was a very, small boat, with a very, small motor and I, a non-swimmer, with no life-jacket was a little apprehensive. But, we soon turned down another small water course and as we moved slowly along the bank Chedo signalled us to be silent. We sat quietly and watched a colony of kingfishers, which were flitting between the water and their nests in the riverbank. I would have felt privileged to have seen one and here were so many pairs, perhaps thirty or forty, I lost count. Their brilliant blue and gold forms flashed between the bank and the water. They flitted from one to the other while above us the canopy of trees overhead allowed only a small amount of sunlight to spread a muted, dappled light and the Kingfishers seemed oblivious to us. A truly wondrous sight!

We made our way back to the landing stage and from there to the headquarters of the Administrators of the reserve. Chedo told us that indeed we had been privileged to have had such an experience because much of the reserve closed to everyone except the botanists and other experts employed by the reserve or, game hunters. They were actively seeking foreign huntsmen, as significant contributors to the reserve's revenue and had hoped that we would promote this form of tourism for them. I was horrified, even though he explained to me that regular culling helped the herds of deer and sounders of wild boar. As soon as their pricing structure for the hunters was raised and then the discussions about 12 pointers, meaning the size of antlers, and gold, silver or bronze trophy kills, I lost interest. I couldn't help it; I fail to understand how anyone can kill an animal for pleasure. In deference to our hosts, who had gone to so much trouble to promote the reserve, we now listened and then asked some pertinent questions. We enquired if they were interested in organizing guided tours, or perhaps some birdwatchers or similar, which they were not.

Nowadays, our friend Chedo has retired and is devastated by the neglect now visited upon the area. Not a form of neglect which would leave the reserve as it once was, in peace and tranquillity. More the form that allows too many tourists and tour organizers who are careless or uncaring of the particular requirements of the flora and fauna of this most spectacular of national treasures. Some years later the Croatian government talked of building a dam on the River Drava, near Osijek. This dam would directly impact on Kopachski Rit and could have catastrophic consequences for the wildlife there. One can but hope that sanity will prevail and that this magnificent area will not disappear forever, sacrificed in the interests of cheaper Electricity.

Some weeks after our guests had left we were taken to visit yet another wine cellar by the Belje Company, who was keen to seek a British partner for their food and wine exports. They bitterly complained that they were currently only receiving 7p a litre for their wines. Under the terms of previous agreements, they were forced to sell their product to one of the other Federal States of Yugoslavia for a fixed price. However, now, under new legislation they were free to try to obtain a real market price.

We went first to see the vast vineyards growing on the gently sloping hills of Southern Baranja, which, according to local legend, had been planted around 98. A.D by the Roman legions of Emperor Trajan to produce wine for his troops to drink instead of the local water, for Baranja at that time, was swampland and infested with malaria-carrying mosquitoes. Then they took us to Knezevi Vinogradi, (meaning Duke's or Emperor's vineyard.) We had friends living here and so this was not my first visit to the village, but I was in for a huge surprise! The building housing the headquarters of the Belje wine division of their company was very unremarkable. I assumed we were to have yet another meeting until they led into a small building, through a doorway, leading to a ladder which disappeared into the earth beneath us. Intrigued, Ilija and I descended the ladder and found ourselves standing in an enormous wine cellar some 8 to ten metres underground. Here stood rows of wooden vats where the wines were aged. The manager proudly showed us along the rows and allowed us small tastings of some of the wines. He explained the process and when I asked him when the cellar had been made he simply shrugged and said it had been there 'forever,' or, according to legend, from Roman times. He was tremendously proud of his wines as were all the people we met there. They invited us to lunch with them before we left and we promised to work as hard as we could to identify and arrange meetings with prospective investors.

Sadly, before this could happen the civil war overtook us and I have no idea which side the people we met, chose to support.

Belje, this huge company was entirely destroyed during the fighting and ceased to exist. We have heard that its lands lay barren and uncultivated, production plants closed down and silent. Baranja is without its little farming communities as once again the villages lie almost empty except for a few elderly residents. Only the Hungarian communities have survived, mainly intact, for most of the Serbs cannot return, and most of the Croats do not want to. It is an interesting fact that once the Croatian villagers had a taste of City life, where they had fled during the conflict, many were not at all keen to return to the arduous and uncertain life of a farmer. I do so hope that the wine production continues and that nothing touched either those ancient vineyards or that amazing wine cellar and those of the private growers and producers.

CHAPTER SIX

In the autumn of 1989, there were discernible changes amongst our friends, especially noticeable at our regular dinner parties. Discussions began regarding the collapse of the Yugoslavian federation because Slovenia and Croatia, in particular, were urgently seeking to become independent states. The rumbling of discontent started at the end of the previous year, and now they were becoming more insistent. But, so far, nothing had intruded into our peaceful and happy existence, except perhaps that Ilija was away from home more often and especially during the evenings. Up to now this had never been a problem, but now he became unwilling to tell me where he had been or with whom he had been. I bit my tongue, but the old demons were returning, reminding me that I had been foolishly trusting of my previous relationships. Was Ilija going to betray my trust too?

I was due to go to England again and so in November, I flew back to London. There awaited me a joyful reunion with my mother, who was always waiting at the arrivals gate for me with other family members. We would go directly to the car and within minutes out would come bags of favourite sweets, sandwiches, and a flask of coffee. Would I like to wait for the first services where I could smoke if I wanted to? Sherbet lemons, Everton mints, and Murray mints were consumed in great quantities until Mum declared eating more would be greedy. She died at the ripe old age of 93 in 2011, and I dread the arrival gate now. Looking on at others being greeted by eager and welcoming arms can be the loneliest experience in the world. Eyes that scan my face swiftly move on in their search for their loved ones.

I thoroughly enjoyed all the preparations for the coming Christmas in Coventry, helping with the making of the mountains of mince pies and sausage rolls. The family now began to gather for a huge party we planned at a local hotel on December 23rd for the celebration of our parents 50th wedding anniversary. My brother, Simon, with his family, travelled down from London. He was an incredibly kind person a solicitor who worked endlessly for the rights of workers, the disabled or those he considered oppressed; he was also a very generous son. He wrote a most touching letter to our parents thanking them for their loving support throughout all his life and particularly education. My father had never been a wealthy man but had somehow always provided whatever we needed. Now Simon would present them with gifts and holidays which delighted them. I was never quite sure what his opinion of me was. He unhesitatingly gave me tremendous support whenever I sought it. However, I often detected a raised eyebrow! He had a most intelligent and lovely wife called Marianne, who was a close friend and two charming daughters who made the visit all the more enjoyable.

Before he left, he took me to aside and told me that he was aware of the tensions in Yugoslavia and was I safe? He also offered any support I may need and told me not to hesitate to contact him should I need anything. I took him up on this offer the following year with a somewhat hilarious shopping trip. I was so grateful that none of them enquired too much about my plans and seemed just happy to see me, especially my parents. Amongst all the joy of Christmas, I missed Ilija intensely, and now I just wanted to get back to him in time to spend the Orthodox Christmas and New Year together. Despite feeling under immense pressure to stay in England, I left for Yugoslavia on the 5th January 1990. My father was obviously unwell, although none realised just how ill he was.

Back in Osijek, Ilija and I were regular visitors to a friend's apartment in Borovo Selo, which today in Croatia, where there was a huge tyre factory. She was one of the head chemists there and was the most engaging person. She immediately took me under her wing and delighted in teaching me the Bosnian-style cookery she had learned in her youth. I marvelled at the enormous, tree-like hibiscus plant she had in the sitting room of her apartment which always produced a single flower, followed by another single flower as the first faded and died. It also received an egg yolk once a week, much to Ilija's amusement. We spent many happy evenings there together, and she was always dismissive of Ilija's warnings as to his concerns about the future for Serbs in Baranja. By the following July in 1990, she had lost her job at the local company. She came to see us in Osijek and looked to be in complete shock. She told of how her assistant at work had announced to her the previous day that he was now the new chief and she was no longer required. Furthermore, all future employees of the company were to be Croatian. The new order was Croatia for Croatians; there was no room for Serbs. The assistant was neither employed as a personnel officer nor did he possess a doctorate or professorship as she. Regardless of all, she explained, she was escorted from the premises, and with no right of appeal had lost her job of over 15 years. She sobbed as she told us and I, who had still not fully comprehended just what was beginning to happen, was shocked and appalled. Ilija, on the other hand, was just very solemn and thoughtful.

Nada was the first of a steady stream of friends who had similar stories to tell. And she was also one of many who were now leaving Baranja, Slavonia, and Croatia to go and live in Serbia, too afraid to stay where most of them were born and bred. Doctors and a surgeon from Osijek hospitals and clinics, teachers, and lecturers from Osijek schools and the university had now lost their jobs. The director of Auto Slavonia, the company that Ilija and I had done so much work with through our agency and in fact from every walk of life, friends of ours were losing their jobs. They all had one thing in common. They were ethnic Serbs, Roma or other nationality, what they were not, were ethnic Croatians. Others left of their own volition because the new regime had re-introduced a document which had first been introduced by the wartime Ustashe government regarding employment. Anyone seeking employment had to sign a declaration of loyalty to Croatia as a condition of employment.

Another chilling re-introduction was the flag which the Ustashe had flown while fighting for Hitler. Most of the Western press seemed ignorant of this and ignored this move. I wondered if they would have ignored a newly unified Germany flying a swastika. So, who were this new government? I had thought that Yugoslavia was slowly evolving into either a Federation of democratically run states or, perhaps would become independent countries, which on the surface did not seem to be a very viable economic alternative. With what cynicism did a Germany that had now reunified, given such active support to Croatia and support the breakup of the Yugoslavian federation into six, small and possibly economically unviable states?

In the early summer of 1989, a political organisation was born in a little shack in Zagreb. Formed in secrecy with one Franjo Tudjman at its head the new party of HDZ was born. Franjo Tudjman was an ex-army officer and self-styled historian who called himself, Doctor Tudjman. To be validated as a historian and moreover, to become the director of the Institute for The History of worker's movement in Croatia, he realised that he required a doctorate which was duly obtained. However, it was later to be claimed that Tudjman plagiarized his doctoral thesis from magazine articles and another's work, and was expelled from the Institute, forcing him to retire from his position there in 1967.

Entitled or not, he kept his title of Doctor and now worked towards becoming Dr. Franjo Tudjman the President of Croatia. Tudjman's rewriting of the history of Yugoslavia from a Croatian perspective brought him into conflict with other historians, and his extreme nationalistic views were now easy to see. It was in his article called 'Wasteland of history' in which he tries to argue that the sufferings of the Jews in the 2nd World War were exaggerated. He further asserts that while there were some deaths, the reports of over 770,000 deaths of Jews, Roma, Serbs and Croatian and other dissidents in the Ustashe death camps were also greatly exaggerated. Despite both German and Allied detailed reports on these death camps. Tudjman also concurs with the conclusions of the Croatian historian Ciliga1898-1992. Ciliga claimed that the Croatian Ustashe fascist regime of 1941-1945, which had boasted that not a single gypsy was alive and living in Croatia after their ethnic cleansing, should have been reformed not destroyed.

Tudjman offered the following quotes from Ciliga as an example of Jewish behaviour in the Ustashe, extermination centres. The Jews 'jealously kept a monopoly of the management and took the initiative in provoking, not only individual but also, mass slaughter of the non-Jews, Communists, Partisans, and Serbs.'

It was little wonder that when the new President of Croatia, Tudjman made public his plans for a new constitution in June 1990 that a sense of dread was felt by many. They feared what they perceived as ominous signs of the old fascist Ustashe state on the rise. Tudjman did nothing to dispel their anxiety. He oversaw the creation of illegal political paramilitary units which challenged the regular army of a Federal Yugoslavia. The minor parties in the new government were the SDP (Socialist Democrat Party) and SDS (The Serbian Democratic Party). There were other smaller parties including the IDS (Istria Democratic Party) which controlled the Istrian peninsular. Thanks in large part to their influence the majority of Istrian Serbs did not suffer the fate of those in the rest of Croatia. However, the three most influential political parties in the new Croatia were all extreme right wing parties. These were HDZ (Croatian Democratic Union,) the HSP (Croatian Loyalist Party,) and the HSS (Croatian Peasant Party). The HDZ and HSP had paramilitary wings of the party. The HDZ wing called ZNG (Army of the National Guard) or Zengi; they were to form the nucleus of the new Croatian Army. The HSP paramilitary wing was called HOSS (Croatian armed force). These paramilitaries appeared when the legal army for all the federal states which made up Yugoslavia was still the J.N.A (Yugoslavian National Army.)

In June 1990, following the elections, these paramilitaries began to appear in the streets of Croatia. The first time I saw them Ilija and I were shopping and noticed four or five men dressed in black military uniforms carrying machine pistols. They were chatting to a couple of the ordinary police force dressed in blue uniforms. Their appearance was so unexpected and strange that we both stopped and stared. They strutted arrogantly along the High Street and from now on this now became a familiar sight.

Jadranka and Zvonko were a highly successful, business couple that Ilija and I had met in 1988. They had a thriving business producing ceramics from their new, modern factory. Most unusually at that time, they employed a nanny for their brood. Zvonko had contacted our agency with regards to the export of his products, and our friendship evolved from the meetings we had. We became regular house guests of theirs and them ours and seemed to have a great deal in common, including music, opera and literature. They were extremely friendly, and we enjoyed their company. They had four charming children who we often met and even on occasions Ilija went sailing with on the Danube. I have never been a great fan of water sports unless as a spectator from the safety of the bank. We had never discussed politics other than the hope that customs barriers would ease and that his company exports would increase.

One evening in September of 1990, after the election of President Tudjman in Croatia, Jadranka and Zvonko came for dinner to our house in Osijek. As we relaxed on large, floor cushions, Jadranka suddenly announced that they had some fantastic news! I wondered if she were pregnant and felt a twinge of envy, how I yearned for a child! Instead of announcing that, her important news was that her eldest son Darko was soon to join the new Croatian army, as soon as he was 18! Before either Ilija or I could comment she added, 'We can prove three generation, clean Croatian blood! Only such men can be accepted! At last, it will be Croatia for Croatians, I am so proud, and he will be paid one hundred Deutschmarks a day! What do you think about that isn't it tremendous news!'

I was speechless and waited as Ilija translated word for word what she had said so that there was no mistake. Zvonko looked at Ilija and got the reaction that he must have expected. Ilija's face had suddenly hardened, and he stared at Zvonko, who was obviously avoiding his gaze. I turned to Jadranka and horrified, I told her 'You can't be serious! That is fascism! How on earth can you think such a primitive principle is wonderful! You will alienate all your Serbian friends!' Everyone stood up, Zvonko and Jadranka were defensive and irritated. I remember Jadranka dismissing my reaction by telling me that because I was a foreigner I didn't understand. They swept out leaving us and our home never to return. Ilija and I were deeply shocked and upset. Then Ilija said 'this is the beginning of the nightmare breakup of Yugoslavia of which I have been warning. You keep telling me I am crazy, as do some of our other friends, but now we all need to be afraid. Because when otherwise normal people talk about ethnic pureness the way they just did, what do you think the extremists will do to all non-Croats now? You heard her, three generation, clean, Croatian blood, Croatia for Croatians.'

And for us, so it began. Although I honestly have to admit that I still had not grasped the seriousness of the situation. I was much more concerned with the increasing amount of time Ilija spent away from our home, and it was becoming a real issue between us. I like to think that I am not a particularly, jealous person. However, now the green-eyed monster had raised its head above the parapet, I was ready to confront the prospect of ending our relationship and returning to the UK. Ilija infuriated me. The only response I could get from him was a flat denial that he was carrying on another relationship accompanied by a flat refusal to tell me what he was doing during his absences. Our agency work was faltering, there was too much uncertainty regarding the future stability for us to consider making promises to investors. I decided to paint the inside of the house and did from the attic to the basement! Even old Mrs. Hrasnici was pleased, and she presented me with some lovely plants for the garden. It didn't help for long, though, and now I was becoming more and more miserable.

Finally, in the middle of September, I told Ilija that I was going back to England and probably wouldn't be returning. His face took on such a look of bewilderment and hurt that I suddenly felt very guilty. Ilija and I were born into the wrong families. Or most people's perception of each other's families. We English, I am told, are cold fish, rarely showing emotions and, generally speaking, unfriendly. Balkan folk, on the other hand, are viewed by non-Balkans as being very noisy, extremely emotional and usually barmy. Barmy in English means a sort of pleasant but, eccentric person rather Monty-Pythonish I suppose. To prove that generalisations are not sensible views, I shout and scream like a fishwife when upset while Ilija stays calm and practical. He arrived home that evening with some flowers and a brown cardboard box. Inside the box were two tiny, grey, Persian kittens. He had found them dumped near a video hire shop we regularly used. 'I just couldn't leave them there' He said. And so began our history of rescuing abandoned creatures!

As we fed and tended them Ilija, at last, explained his absences. He began by saying that the situation in Croatia was becoming extremely grave and potentially very dangerous.Tudjman and his politicians were using the same rhetoric as fascist Ustashe parties had used in 1941. I had no idea what this meant, and so we spent that evening and many others to follow discussing the history of the area. The relationship between Croatia and Baranja and then between the different federal states which made up Yugoslavia. I began to watch the Croatian news on television and saw the rallies with the flag waving; there was a jingoistic nationalism evident in this media coverage. I was appalled by the behaviour of the Catholic Church in Croatia too. Altar candles swathed in Croatian flags, as they blessed rows of paramilitaries parading more of the flags. I thought that their role should now be one of reconciliation, not harbingers of war eagerly supporting the extremists urgency for action. They seemed to be very influential in Croatia at this time. We also had visits from friends of ours who were ethnic Croatians. They too were horrified at the prospect of ethnic cleansing in their state, the continuous emphasis on ethnicity deeply troubled them. Tudjman's rallying cry of Croatia for Croatians was deliberately designed to play to an audience of all right-wing ethnic Croatians. With increasing concerns over a shrinking economy and rising inflation and unemployment, HDZ propaganda proclaimed that the Serbs were to blame for Croatia's looming financial crisis. This, because ethnic Serb-Croatians held all the best jobs, undeservedly in their view. By no means all Croatians supported the HDZ, the problem was they either did not have a voice or, possibly due to intimidation, were unwilling to oppose the extremists publicly.

In this climate, ethnic Serbs living in Croatia and Baranja were now holding unofficial meetings to discuss the situation. I have to admit that I thought Ilija was being overly dramatic when he shared his fears of a catastrophic break-up of Yugoslavia. I argued that it was inconceivable that he would be fighting our friends and what about Franjo and all the other ethnically mixed families? What about the children of these marriages, would they have to choose? 'All you are saying is true,' he said. 'But the bombing of Serbian shops, cars, cafés and business premises is happening, and no one is trying to either prevent it or arrest the criminals.' Although reported on all the television news services the phrase, 'nepoznati pochinioci,' meaning 'the perpetrators are unknown' was always used. The anti-Serb campaign orchestrated by the HDZ slowly gained momentum. Another chilling reminder of a fascist, pre-war Germany came with the burning of Serbian books and paintings in towns all across Croatia by the extremists.

Early one morning in late September Ilija and I went to my favourite piazza which was close to our home. Things had changed since those first happy days of living in the City. A little stall, where we often bought a hamburger type snack called chevapi, closed, its Albanian owner was gone. But more shockingly was the sight that greeted us in the middle of the market. There was an enormous pyre of books and paintings which were still smoking and burning in the early morning gloom and so it must have been carried out during the previous night or early morning. Ilija approached the fire, ashen-faced and furiously angry he quietly cursed. Of the passersby some glanced curiously at the sight, some passed with faces averted while others were staring in horror. There were piles of burned books by Serbian authors and poets amongst them a holder of the Nobel prize; Ivo Andrich and Desanka Maximovich and Vuk Karadzich.

A painting by Momor Kapor lay half-burnt but still smouldering and there too were books by Croatian anti-fascist writers like Miroslav Krleza. Can we save any? I asked Ilija. But he didn't answer me, and we stood and watched as the books slowly burned. Such a huge pile of books perhaps over a thousand made me ask from where on earth they had all come. Ilija's answer was that he supposed that because there were so many, they were probably from the schools, colleges, and the university. And that HDZ member would almost certainly have burnt theirs not wanting to appear unpatriotic and to be found with those books on their bookshelves.

Slowly, at first, historical complaints and resentment, imagined or real, were stoked and gradually became inflamed. Tensions were now increasing on a daily basis. I saw the demonstrations on television outside the Yugoslavian Army barracks in Croatia. It was so strange, so surreal it was almost mundane. We went about as usual, shopping, meeting friends, Croatian friends, Serbian friends and Roma friends. We watched the news, saw the new uniforms parading around on the streets, but hey, nothing could happen. It was just a crazy transition. The new political parties were many people's first dalliances with politics and political freedom.

We helped with the harvest in Cheminac as usual, and we were there for the making of sausages, salami and all kinds of spiced meats, smoked hams and hocks. Quite an event; Ilija would signal to me that, very shortly, the pigs would be shot with a humane killer. Quickly disappearing into the farmhouse, I would turn the volume of the radio up or put my fingers in my ears, or both The men saw to the cleaning of the animals, removing the hair from its skin, the entrails and the butchering. All carried out under the supervision of an experienced butcher who came to his friend's farm to help. He was usually given a large joint of meat to take home as a reward. The women meanwhile prepared and served endless cups of coffee, beer, plum brandy and water to the men as they toiled. This preparation of the meat for winter could only take place, when the temperatures had plummeted to around zero, usually in the last week of November or early December. There is much stamping of feet and numbed fingers warmed over an open fire. One of the men will bring in the fresh liver and lung to be prepared with garlic and with hunks of fresh bread and then served for breakfast mid-morning. Some of the women begin to clean the skins of the intestines ready for the making of the sausages. Others organize the cooking of the skin which is going make delicious crackling. The lady of the house is usually ensconced in her warm kitchen. There, with a small army of women helpers some making salovnjak, a suet pastry, filled with their damson jam and doughnuts. Oh, how I loved these cakes! Others are busy preparing lunch to be enjoyed in the late afternoon. Finally, the meat cut into chops, hams, ribs, minced meat or schnitzels is packed away. The sausages, kulen and stuffed stomachs (not dissimilar to haggis) and the rest of the meat to be smoked, set aside. A huge vat is full of boiling liquid, cooking the skin which gradually transforms into crackling. After removing this crispy speciality, made from the skin, the lard is poured into large metal vessels. As soon as everything has been cleaned and put away, the freshly cooked sausage and pork chops appear with delicious cakes and more freshly baked bread. The men joke and laugh, sometimes arguing over their work because there was always one who knew better than the others. The women on the other had been firmly under the thumb of the of the farmer's wife. It was her kitchen, and no one questioned her recipes or decisions! My role in this, at first, was the chief washer-upper and then later I graduated to the art of cleaning the intestines. My grandfather had been a butcher, and my mother had made faggots and sausages in his shop before her marriage. She later gave me the recipes for them, and I still make them whenever I can.

The chardaks and Winter store cupboards were filling up. Tomato sauce was made and bottled, pickled gherkins, peppers, beetroot and mixed winter salads are all prepared. Large bunches of dried herbs and peppers were ready for the store room having hung outside under the eaves of the houses for several months. There were sacks of potatoes, huge pumpkins and squash and many strings of onions and garlic all packed into the storerooms. Root vegetables lay in trays of dry soil and bags of lima beans, of walnuts and hazelnuts were hung to dry before being shelled, it had been a good harvest this year. Then there were the relishes, ajvar, a delicious chutney-like mix of red peppers, aubergines, onion, and garlic. It can be as fiery as any vindaloo curry or mild enough for even the smallest children to enjoy. Large plastic containers packed with salted white cabbage used well into the following spring as a salad or for sarma, (cabbage rolls). I have always enjoyed the way we only eat fresh food that is in season here. We look forward to the first tomatoes of the season because neither of us enjoys the out of season, tasteless hybrids! Franjo showed me his impressive stock of smoked, freshly made sausage, hocks, and legs of pork, called sunka, hanging in his loft and he generously kept us well-supplied during the winter. Although there was a small opening to allow a steady flow of fresh air, it was covered in mesh and protected this precious store from thieves. Not the two-legged variety, unless you include birds, but four-legged. Franjo had a large, black tom-cat who usually spent his days reclining in a wicker shopping basket. A most superior creature he did not welcome any show of affection. He kept the farm mostly free of rodents and divided his time between his three favourite pastimes of hunting, eating or sleeping. He suddenly began to gain weight at an alarming rate and was soon searching for a larger basket. A mystified family looked on in amazement until a visit from an irate neighbour. This man had been unwise enough to leave his loft window unprotected and thus his smoked meats of which 12 large sausages were missing. They offered reparation, and it was accepted, and the black beast gradually regained his former weight. Everyone except Franjo and the aggrieved neighbour thought this amusing. Perhaps it's a particular talent of black cats. My Mother often told the story of her fortuitous intervention when she caught her black cat trying to drag the Christmas turkey, out through the cat door. The cat had grabbed it from the kitchen worktop, where Mum had been stuffing it, and only its size saved it. Mother retrieved her 10 kg turkey, finished stuffing it, rubbed it with salt and hoped that a long roasting would prevent the cats participation in its preparation from infecting anyone. She didn't share the story with us until after dinner.

It was time for me to go to England again. To go Christmas shopping and buy the other things that I couldn't find in Osijek, such as Tabasco sauce, treacle and if there is room in the case, brown sauce and a few cat treats! I had left the packed case by the door, sometimes I took two with me but had decided on one this time. On my arrival at Heathrow, I lifted my suitcase from the baggage carousel and immediately knew something was very wrong. It was so light that I opened it there and then and saw that it was empty. I rushed across to the lost and found and reported my problem. They were very kind and after several telephone calls told me that they would be going immediately to the baggage handlers area to conduct a search. In spite of my turmoil, I explained that I just could not wait to find out the result because my family was waiting for me at the arrival gate. They took all my details and advised me that I should not worry, that I could leave, and they would let me know what their results of their investigations were, the next day at the latest. My family was indeed there to greet me, and I tearfully explained about the suitcase, and they were suitably sympathetic. As soon as I reached home, I rang Ilija. I told him of my great misfortune but, Ilija cheerily replied that I hadn't lost anything. Why? Because I had not taken the right suitcase, the kind friend who had been there to wish me bon voyage had carried the bag to the car, the one I had left by the bedroom door. He should have taken the one on the bed, but no one told him that, perhaps they didn't I thought, but what sort of idiot doesn't realize that a packed suitcase is usually, heavy. He had also accompanied us to the airport and had been the one to hand the bags over at the check-in desk. Well, at least, I hadn't lost anything! Luckily I had been given a contact number for the baggage control at Heathrow terminal two and explained what had happened apologizing profusely for causing such a fuss. The airport representative was charming and, in turn, thanked me for admitting it was my mistake. Some people don't admit that they said! Fortunately, for me, I still have lots of clothes at my home in the UK.

I spent a most happy time with the family before returning to Croatia in early December, with several suitcases crammed with goodies and Christmas gifts for family and friends. And one of my Mum's Christmas puddings which, not only found themselves on Serbia plates but also American, because my brother used to take one home to America with him too. Although my Father appeared to be a little frailer, he did seem to be recovering his health. I barely had time to unpack my suitcases.Within days, I was on my way back to Coventry. Jude had called me to say that her husband had died suddenly. She and Fred had been getting ready to go to a Christmas office party, and while Jude was taking a shower, Fred had been reading his newspaper. She found him, lifeless, the paper still in his hands, sitting in his favourite chair. Judith's neighbours had found her in the middle of the main road where she had stood screaming in shock and anguish. I stayed with her for the next few weeks, helped her with all the arrangements and we cried and laughed together at the memories of the times we had all shared as close friends. Fred had been a dear, sweet, gentle giant of a man of 65 and about to retire. Ruled by two little Chihuahuas, who were spoilt tyrants called Monty and Python, after Fred had painstakingly cooked chicken for them (when they wanted it not before), they were known to bite his fingers as he offered them titbits. All Fred would ever say was 'Now then lads, be nice to your old dad.' He was one of the kindest and soft-hearted people I ever knew, and Jude was utterly bereft without him. I hated to leave her now but there was little alternative.

CHAPTER SEVEN

On January 4th, 1991, I boarded my flight to Croatia. It is always hard to say goodbye to your family and friends. To live in a different country to one's own is akin to having one leg in each! I had missed Ilija dreadfully and yet I wanted to give Jude all the support she needed, for as long as she wanted me to remain by her side. I left with the promise that should she need me I would answer the call! In any event, I would be returning within a couple of months for one of my regular visits. Visa restrictions by Yugoslavia at this time were complicated and limited the length of the visa. Moreover, I had to apply for a new one each time I made the journey. Life would have been a lot simpler were Ilija, and I married, but I wasn't ready yet, and there was still a divorce to be finalized. Ilija was waiting for me at the arrival gate, and as we hugged each other, I realized that I never wanted to be anywhere else in the World but inside his encircling arms. And when I arrived home there was a third little kitten who welcomed me. While Ilija was opening his car door one evening, he looked down to see a tiny tabby cat sitting on his foot. Naturally, he picked her up and she had found her home. He called her Bubica meaning ladybird, and from that moment on.she became his shadow

The day after I arrived I had my suitcases lying open in our bedroom at the front of the house when there was a knock on the door. I opened it to see an old Roma lady standing there. She asked for some water, so I walked through to our sitting room, into the kitchen at the rear of the house to fetch it. I came back to find her standing in the hall outside the bedroom door. I gave her the water and a little money and she left. We never locked our doors in those days, either in Osijek or the village and so I just closed the door without turning the key. Unfortunately, for me, a friend chose to call me, and I took the phone into the kitchen so that I could make some coffee as we chatted. A little later I saw to my surprise that the front door was open. I thought Ilija had returned, and I went into the bedroom where the sight of my suitcases laying open and ransacked greeted me; my purse was empty of the five hundred pounds I had brought from England. The contents of my jewellery box lay scattered across the floor. Gone were all my earrings, bracelet and gold necklaces, but worse than all gone were the wedding rings that Ilija and I had purchased in Holland and had engraved ready for our marriage. Fortunately, Ilija walked in at that moment and took charge. He called the police, who told him that the person they suspected was the culprit was still in the street outside. But, she had long ago passed the stolen items to an accomplice, and we had no chance of recovering anything. I tried to be philosophical about the robbery. I had been careless, most of the items were replaceable, and I sincerely hoped that whoever used our rings for their marriage would have the most miserable life! I have never felt any significant attachment to possessions, except for those given to me by people I loved. And it had solved the problem of whether or not I should continue to wear the jewellery that my first husband had bought me! We went to Cheminac the next day to spend the Christmas break with the family, and although I was still feeling upset, we didn't tell them about the robbery. Ilija said that they would be deeply upset and ashamed, that such a thing could happen to a visitor to Yugoslavia.

Barely had our Serbian Christmas celebrations ended when one evening in January there was a knock on our door and into the room came three men wearing black uniforms. The same uniforms that we had seen worn by the men who had appeared so recently strutting about in the centre of the town. All were relatively young, perhaps mid-twenties and were carrying automatic guns. All were unsmiling, and I immediately sensed that Ilija had become very tense. He invited them to sit, which they did, taking the chairs while Ilija and I sat on the sofa.

'What do you want?' said Ilija very curtly in a manner I had never seen him use with anyone before.

'We are checking on her,' one of them replied. 'She is a stranger, and we have the right to ensure that she is living at the address that we have in our records at our police headquarters.'

'Well, you can see for yourself that she is and if there is nothing else you may leave' said Ilija.

Totally ignoring Ilija, one, who had some stripes denoting his rank on his shoulders, turned to me and said in poor English 'Do like Croatia?'

'Yes,' I replied, and I wondered about offering them some coffee. Ilija must have read my mind and said to them 'If there is nothing else we can say goodnight.'

Again ignoring Ilija, the one with stripes asked me 'And friends, do you lot friends?'

'Yes, thank you I have made a lot of friends' I said. None of them showed the slightest sign relaxing or being as friendly as the other local policeman I had met, which only increased the alarm I was now beginning to feel. The man with stripes now attempted more complex English sentences which I could not understand. I thought he was asking me who my friends were. Ilija intervened and told me that he was indeed asking me for the names of my friends and what did I think of new Croatia? I could hear the fury in Ilija's voice; these were not casual enquiries they were demands for me to name my friends. I told Ilija to inform him that it was nothing to do with him who my friends were or what my opinions about Croatia were. That my visa was in order, and I had registered with the aliens department at the local police station. As Ilija finished translating what I had said, one of the group now began to click the safety catch on and off on his gun. The man with the stripes stood up to face Ilija, who was also standing. Ilija was furious that they were trying to frighten us. There were angry words exchanged between them. Everyone else stood up, and I was so afraid that they would attack Ilija, that I now moved quickly towards our telephone, telling Ilija that I was going to call my embassy in Zagreb to complain about this harassment. I could barely speak because I thought my heart would beat out of my chest, but I was determined not to let them see just how afraid I was. Ilija smiling now, which I knew meant trouble, asked the Blackshirt, who was still clicking the safety catch of his gun on and off. 'Why are you doing that? Is it because I am a Serb, an Orthodox Serb, are you trying to threaten me. Do you think I should be afraid of you? The blackshirt didn't answer, and I picked up the telephone and said 'Ilija where is the number for the British Zagreb Ambasada (embassy).' I knew I had to break the impasse. The man with stripes who appeared to be their leader turned on his heels and walked out of the door without another word, followed by the other two. One of them yelled from the garden gate that they would visit us again whenever they wished to check my whereabouts.

Ilija and I just sat and hugged each other. 'Now you see for the first time what these Zengi are really like, don't you?' said Ilija 'They are Tudjman's dogs who he has set loose to terrorize innocent people. Now do you see how dangerous they are?' We agreed to go and complain about this visit to the police chief in Osijek whose name was Josip Reihl-Kir. The next day we went to the Police headquarters in Osijek and with only a minimum of delay were shown into the office of Chief Reihl-Kir. There were two other senior officers with him. All were in civilian dress and were exceptionally kind and welcoming. They listened patiently to our story and also that we had a successful agency and were bringing business and investment to the area. That we would hesitate to host any more visits by these investors and buyers until we could be confident of their security. Chief Reihl-Kir promised us that he would investigate the circumstances of our complaint and that we should have no further worries because the incident would not happen again. Our impression was that these three high-ranking officers were genuinely concerned about what had happened. What tragedy was soon to unfold regarding this police chief, the most decent of human beings.

Chief Reihl-Kir showed tremendous heroism at this time. He must at heart have been a pacifist for he not only expressed a most earnest desire for peace in public but, also acted on that belief. He predicted his assassination in reports to his superiors in Zagreb. After our meetings, we heard more of him because he made visits to Serbian villages begging people, not to be provoked into fighting because he wanted to find a peaceful solution. We knew there were other reasonable men like him. They too were trying to prevent men like Branimir Glavash from fermenting hatred and planning the killing of Serbs and fellow Croats in Osijek. Glavash used to appear on local television news programmes urging his supporters to be proud of their Ustashe heritage and not to be afraid to announce proudly to the whole World that they were Ustashe! Both Ilija and I knew Glavash. We regularly had dinner at a local restaurant and Glavash was always there playing cards. He wasn't employed, and I thought he was a professional gambler. However, he was often drunk and so I remember wondering how successful he was in his card games. We also frequently saw Tomislav Kralj there. Ilija once paid his bar tab because Kralj was drunkenly arguing with a waiter that he had already paid it. He had been about to be arrested when Ilija felt pity for him. Kralj became an avid HDZ supporter and eventually became part of Franjo Tudjman's inner circle of cohorts.With the rise in fortunes of the HDZ so did those of Glavash, and he became one of the local bully boys, eventually becoming the Osijek chief of police after the assassination of Josef Reihl-Kir.

Chief Reihl-Kir was travelling in an unmarked police car to a meeting with the local Serbs in Tenja a village about 5km South of Osijek. They had erected barricades as a defence against the constant attacks by Croatian paramilitary groups orchestrated by the likes of Glavash and others. The Chief's car stopped at a Croatian police roadblock and one of those manning it, a reservist Croatian policeman called Anton Gudelj, opened fire. Chief Reihl-Kir suffered 16 bullets wounds and died instantly. Two of the local Serbs, accompanying the Chief to the meeting, were also killed along with the Croatian driver. A third Serbian passenger was severely wounded. The Chief had chosen to go to the meeting without an escort in order not to provoke the Serbs he was to meet. Gudelj fled to Austria and was eventually arrested and indicted. After the civil war, despite him fleeing to Austria, Glavash was arrested and imprisoned but, only handed a relatively short sentence for the brutal beatings and murders he had orchestrated and taken part in of both Serbian and Croatian civilians in Osijek. Most of these criminals were eventually released, following an amnesty, having served very short sentences.

However, before the events above unfolded, earlier, in late January 1991 and about two weeks after the first visit by the Zengi or paramilitary units of the HDZ party, there came another knock at our door. This time, there were two of these black shirts, armed, but not as aggressive as the first had been. Apart from greeting me courteously, they did not ask me any questions or speak to me. They spoke rapidly to Ilija as if explaining something and when they had finished, Ilija could not conceal his amusement. 'Did you understand what they just said?' He asked me, and then as I shook my head, he continued, 'those Zengi that came to see you and made threats, were not in fact Zengi. They were Serbians, who had got hold of some Zengi uniforms. Their intention was to make you think badly of Zengi forces!' The two Blackshirts were not impressed by our mirth and now began to talk to him in a different vein. Their masks slipped, and they became aggressive, almost spitting their words out. I didn't need Ilija to translate their threats.

After they left Ilija suggested that now was the time to telephone the British Consulate, in Zagreb, which I did. And what a strange experience that was! A woman answered the phone at the British Consulate in Zagreb. She had an accent, and so I asked her if she were a member of the Consulate because I wanted to speak to the British Consul. She said that the Consul was not there, but I could freely talk to her. I expressed my concern at the manner in which I thought the paramilitary police had behaved. Harassing me on two separate occasions despite promises by the police chief after the first such visit. I also suggested to her that the Black-shirted paramilitaries patrolling the streets reminded me of Hitler's brown-shirts. Her reply stunned me for she said 'We won the election here, and so you will have nothing further to fear, you may live peacefully here without any problem.' I retorted 'What on earth do you mean by saying that we won the election? We are British! It's nothing to do with us' I put down the phone feeling utterly confused. Both Ilija and I now felt that Chief Reihl-Kir had no control over these Zengi forces, and it made us feel very uneasy indeed. I immediately sent a letter of protest to the Foreign Office in London and learned later that the Zagreb Consulate denied that any such conversation between one of their staff and me had ever taken place. But one positive outcome was that the Blackshirts did not return to our home. At least not for a while. Not until after we had escaped.

In late February, we were contacted by an English company who we had earlier sent details of Slavonian Oak products to and now they expressed a wish to place a large order for oak flooring and other products. I urged Ilija to fly to England with the samples and contract proposals. He was not entirely happy with the idea, but I told him that I would go and stay with my friend Rada, which I did. She lived nearby, and so I spent most of my days at home and slept at her flat in the evenings.

Ilija returned after ten days in England in late March, and he was elated because he brought proposals for £1.3 million worth of contracts He arrived just before Easter weekend and with the Orthodox celebrations for Easter beginning the following week we decided not to contact the Croatian company regarding the contract until after both holidays. And because of the events following these celebrations, the contract was never signed, and the English companies were forced to go elsewhere for their order.

We spent Sunday 31st March, the Catholic Easter day, with our friends Peter and Mitzi. This was the last time the four of us were ever together because a little over two weeks later, Ilija and I, had left Osijek forever. And they soon returned to America to live.

A week later on 7th April 1991 and the Orthodox Easter Sunday, we were on our way to Ilija's mother's house in the village of Jagodnjak. We passed a wasteland of tree stumps that had once been an ancient forest of Slavonian oak where the deer who raided the farmer's fields opposite had hidden before making their sorties on the crops. The forest had suddenly been cut down despite vociferous opposition from many of the local people. Slavonian Oak forests were usually almost never cut down en masse. Forest husbandry was a point of pride, and only carefully selected trees removed. It was sad to pass this barren waste, for the trees had been taken as a cash crop no doubt to pay for munitions. However, the sun was shining, and it was going to be another lovely day!

Who could have guessed, on that bright, warm spring morning of 1991, that such acts as neighbours killing neighbours, hundreds of farms abandoned or the shelling of their villages were to being visited upon these people before another Easter Day? Or that such ethnic hatred preached by those with their own, particular agenda would bring the terrors that lay in store for us all? As we turned into Vida's street, we saw all the tables and chairs set out on the road for an enormous street party. The sweet cherry trees in the gardens and lining the street were in full blossom and the neighbours were gathering to enjoy this celebration. The old and young all chattering, laughing and toasting each other with glasses of wine, juices, beers, and plum brandy. There were gaggles of geese, roaming freely over the grass verges and terrorizing anyone who dared get to get too close to them. A cacophony of squealing piglets, snuffling sows, lowing cattle and the insistent crowing of the roosters as they responded to other's challenges as though vying for some champion's title. There were so many smiling faces, and that is an enduring memory for me of that time. I had no idea or cared even less, which of Ilija's friends and family that I was meeting were Croats, Serbs, Roma Gypsies, Hungarians, Czechs, and Poles. Any more than I would have made mental notes about ethnicity when meeting Scots, Irish or Welsh much less, Gaul, Celtic, Viking, Goth, Vandal or Anglo-Saxon peoples in the UK. I had always thought claims of a particular ethnicity in the UK very strange indeed, for who knows from where our ancestors came?

We enjoyed the feasting, singing and dancing until long after dusk as gradually the tables and chairs were reclaimed by their owners until finally, there was just a small group of us remaining. I expected us to leave for home but instead Vida took my arm and leading me towards her house said, 'leave the men to their affairs daughter, they need to talk.' Ilija's mother was a brave little person. She had survived the horrors of German occupation and Ustasa attacks on her village in her native Bosnia during World War Two. She also had a vivid imagination and had recently called the local defence force to report that a Croatian neighbour, with whom she had had a long -running boundary dispute, had a machine gun. Luka, of the local defence force, asked her how she knew that he was armed, and she told him that she could hear him repeatedly cocking and reloading the gun. Invited to describe the sound she said that it was similar to someone playing the accordion. Very wisely, Luka called Ilija who realised that his mother was afraid that all Croatians were now armed and the deep distrust of their proximity, a relic of her wartime sufferings, had again surfaced.

Even in these troubled times, no one dreamt that they would have to leave Baranja. It had become a place of sanctuary and safety for Croatian Serbs. Ilija took me to see a parcel of land of around 2 acres that he had bought from the widowed sister of some friends in Jagodnjak. There we could build our home and future. One of our new neighbours was to be the Janus family. Milan Janus and Ilija were particularly close. His widowed mother was a most remarkable lady. She fed many of the Serbian refugees passing by her farm. These refugee families often came by any means available, and many only had the possessions that they had been able to carry.

The celebration was to be another last time. The last time these neighbours would celebrate Easter Day together sitting beneath the trees. The last time some of them would celebrate Easter Day here because, some had fled to Serbia or, a distant country, Like Dragan or 'Smiler' as I had called him. He was a jovial young father of two, who stood up to see what was happening when he heard gunshots and died immediately from a sniper's shot to his head. His young

wife and children were offered asylum in Canada and left less than
a year later. Dusan, known as Kevas, a sweet soul, who lived in
the world of Doc Holliday and Dodge City, Kansas, found all the
shelling and shooting too much to bear. He committed suicide a few
months later. Ljubisha was murdered by the side of the road when
he had stopped to help someone who flagged him down. It was now
extremely dangerous to venture out of the villages at night. Ambushes
and sniper fire were more prevalent and very real possibility. The day
to day running of their farms had also become a nightmarish labour
of going about their tasks in their fields of planting or reaping while
fearing the very real threat from a sniper's bullet. The insanity of the
situation was to be manifested by Croatian and Serbian workers,
working side by side all day in their factories as if everything were
normal. But, as soon as they returned to their homes the Serbs and
Croatians were each manning their barricades and fortifying their
villages. The minority groups within these villages now moved to
where their ethnicity was in the majority. Serbians living in Croatia
crossed the bridge from Osijek to find refuge in Serbian villages in
Baranja, some Croatians crossed the other way, moving to live in the
city. What began as a slow trickle of Serbians leaving Osijek after
the June 1990 elections in Croatia, became a flood after May 1991.
Then they came from all over Croatia expelled through the pogroms
of the paramilitary wings of the Croatian National parties or they left
in fear of their lives. Some from Northern Croatia took the shortest
route and crossed into Bosnia and then into Serbia.

Now there was the plight of the Baranja families of mixed
ethnicity and the personal tragedies visited upon them. Grandfather
could be ethnically Hungarian with perhaps an ethnically half-
German grandmother. Perhaps, their child would marry a Croatian
or Serbian? Perhaps, their grandchildren would marry an ethnic
Serbian, Croatian or Hungarian or someone of mixed ethnicity?
Before the civil war, everyone had been citizens of Yugoslavia, not
a particular federal state. How were these people of mixed ethnicity
to relate to declaring themselves from one group or another? How
would they be able to live in the New Croatia with Tudjman's battle

cry of 'Croatia for Croatians'? Some married couples separated, many to later divorce, leaving confused and fearful children. One or two Serbs chose to follow their Croatian wives to live in Croatia. One of the worst aspects of this racial profiling visited upon a bemused and fearful population was the effect on their children, especially the young men. We knew many youngsters who had to choose one side or the other. Whichever side they chose, Croatian, or Serbian many became the most extremist of either side. As if they had to prove their worthiness or pride in whichever ethnicity they had chosen. It was extremely troubling that such young people now expressed hatred for the parent of what they deemed to be the shameful side of their birth. We are still in contact with a few of such young men, and all of them have suffered a great deal in the aftermath of the conflict, and very few have made peace with both sides of their family.

Our dear Franjo made a decision which was to cost him dearly in the coming years. In his village of Cheminac, the minority ethnic Serbs living there were becoming increasingly afraid. As tensions mounted and groups of militant Croatian nationalists were roaming the streets of the village terrorizing Serbs or moderate Croatians, he opened his home to them, and many slept there at night. These were people he had grown up with, playing for the same football teams, sharing family celebrations and helping each other with the harvests. Franjo found it incomprehensible that they were suddenly unwelcome members of a predominately Croatian, village community. One night, HOSS wearing their trademark black shirts, a paramilitary group, similar in ideology and actions to Hitler's Brownshirts, came to Franjo's home. They demanded to know if his nephews were there, nephews who were half-Serbian and half Croatian. And they also demanded names of any others sheltering in his house; they were aggressive and threatening. Franjo had met them at the door with his gun drawn and ordered them from his property, having also called the regular police force in Beli Manastir asking them for their protection. The group left but did not forget or forgive that action of Franjo's. There was to be retribution. They would have to wait until the end of 1991 to exact it, but exact it they did.

Around 11 a.m. on the morning of the 17th April 1991, Ilija and I were getting ready to meet the principles of the company regarding a contract for the supply of wood flooring. Ilija had obtained this order on his recent visit to the UK, and he was very excited about it. The telephone rang, Ilija answered it and following a short conversation his whole demeanour changed. 'I have to go to meet someone, and I will probably have to cancel the meeting.' He looked so worried as he told me this, that I immediately realized something was very wrong. It was not the time to make a fuss or question him further, and so I just hugged him and told him to go and not worry about anything else.

I pottered about finding jobs to do because I was concerned for Ilija. I imagined all sorts of things. Was he being prosecuted regarding some traffic offence? He had a penchant for parking wherever the thought he would and was very casual about the changing colours of traffic lights. Was he having an affair with someone and had her husband or boyfriend found out? I had still not recovered my ability to trust the fidelity of the man I loved. I even contemplated how much it would cost me to quarantine our cats should I decide to return to live in England.

Finally, after what seemed an age but, was only about an hour, Ilija returned home. Now he broke the news that we had to leave. We had to leave that night and take everything with us because he doubted we would ever return to this house or Osijek. I was utterly astounded, and now I did begin to question him. What was all this drama? Was he crazy? We had invested so much money in this house, were we now, just going to throw it all away by leaving? What about this contract, we stood to make a lot of money on it? Where would we go? My questions were endless and came rapidly now, one after the other without giving Ilija a chance to respond. He waited for the end of my outburst, took my hands in his and said 'they plan to kill me. Ivan, you know him, he is a Croatian traffic policeman, and he is the one who phoned me earlier. He asked me to meet him at one of our friend's home. He heard from a reliable source that the Zengi, those Blackshirts that came here, will arrest me tomorrow, and I will then disappear.' I was horrified and of course, I immediately set about packing all our belongings into some plastic bags Ilija had bought for the job. We couldn't go and ask for any cardboard boxes from the shops for fear of giving our intentions away. We had some forty plastic bags full of our belongings when we finally finished around 2 a.m the following morning. A lorry was coming to collect us at around 3 a.m, and they would load all our kitchen cupboards, fridges, chairs, settees, and tables, etc., along with the plastic bags. I fervently hoped that there would be enough room in the lorry take everything. We had spent a lot of money furnishing our home.

Exhausted, we collapsed onto the settee and then Ilija asked me where my passport was. Oh dear! I have this dreadful habit of putting things 'in a safe place'. So safe, in fact, that they disappear forever because I have forgotten their very secure location. After the theft of our money and jewellery, I put banknotes in books to keep them secure. The only problem was we had hundreds of books and I could never remember the title of the one acting as a safety deposit box. It drove Ilija raving mad and I had promised to stop the practice. However, the promise came too late for my passport. We now opened all forty sacks and frantically searched for it. Recriminations flew, for my part all Balkan people were barmy lunatics, for Ilija's part all English women and me, in particular, were infuriating, unreasonable and illogical creatures. Having searched all the bags and every other place imaginable we debated how we could cross the bridge into Baranja, in the middle of the night, with possible police checks and me with no identification. Then, my eyes lighted on the cat bed! A sudden urge made me go and lift up the cushion in the bed, and lone behold! My passport!

The lorry arrived on time, and we loaded all our possessions as quickly and quietly as possible. Our little tabby cat ladybird and one of the grey Persian cats were in their pet carrier, and now I went to find our third cat called Prince. Unable to find him I was distraught knowing that I had to leave him behind, there wasn't a minute to lose because the lorry driver was becoming very nervous about hanging around our home for too long. He was afraid a neighbour would report our strange activity to the police. We had to leave and, to our relief, crossed the bridge over the River Drava without incident. Arriving in Jagodnjak around four a.m. we unloaded most of our possessions into a friend's basement. At last, we opened the door to our new temporary home. It was a small house owned by one of Ilija's friends who was working abroad and who offered it to us for as long as we needed it. And I looked around at this nicely furnished comfortable little house and thought that it would be a pleasant place to stay until we returned to our house in Osijek probably within a few weeks. It never crossed my mind for second that I would never see either our house or Osijek ever again, and what is more never wanted to.

The following morning I rang my friend Mitzi in Osijek and explained that we had left unexpectedly and could she please go and feed the little Grey cat we had left behind. I didn't go into details about our reasons for leaving. Mitzi is Croatian, a very kind and sweet friend and I felt awkward about involving her. She rang me back within the hour with some startling news. Mitzi told me rather breathlessly that she couldn't approach our house because Zengi paramilitaries had cordoned it off. She also didn't want to say anything over the telephone, and so again there was no discussion about why we had left.

I am sure that she knew and in fact, she and her Hungarian husband decided not long after this to return to America because they didn't feel safe in Osijek. When we were eventually able to contact them in 1995, she told me that they had returned to Croatia after the war to find that their house occupied by a Zengi officer. However, they were successful in evicting him and his family and sold the house. Now, with great sadness they had gone back to America to live, abandoning their previous plans and shattering the dream they, and so many others, had nursed all their working lives; to save enough to retire on and live comfortably in Yugoslavia.

The literal translation of the Serbian village called Jagodnjak is 'strawberry village.' A small friendly place where everyone knew everyone else. On Sundays and Holy days, worshipers packed the little

Serbian Orthodox church dating from around 1860. In its graveyard lie the generations of Serbians who lived there. The Serbs settled there in around 1663 and farmed the fertile land. Other villages sprang up around Jagodnjak including Cheminac, which almost exclusively populated by Germans, settling there after fleeing the plague in Europe. The other settlements were also either Hungarian, German or Serbian. The Croatians did not reside in the area in any number until after the W.W.2 when they moved into the farms of the German people who had either fled with Hitler's retreating army or forcibly repatriated to Germany. Therefore, when tensions were mounting between the Serbian population and the Croatians, each village, except those of the Hungarians, built barricades and fortified their perimeters. Most especially the Serbians, who were afraid of attacks being launched by the paramilitary forces from Osijek. During this period, the Yugoslavian Army was confined to barracks to prevent them becoming involved in the skirmishes. However, the Croatian paramilitaries had access to field artillery and regularly shelled Jagonjak and other Serb villages, from the Croatian side of the River Drava.

There was occasional sniper fire into the village now, and Ilija asked me not to venture outside unless he was with me. We could still visit our friends and Ilija's mother, even going to Cheminac on one occasion. Franjo warned Ilija not to attempt the journey again because he feared for our safety. I was still in regular contact with my friends in Osijek because the telephone lines were still working. Not long after we arrived in Jagonjak, I rang our home number in Osijek. A male voice answered and in my best Serbian I said 'Jesi li policija?' The man replied 'Da, zasta?' I replied 'Zato to je moj kuca.' Silence from the other end. Now I said 'Bas me briga za kuca, izvolite, ali, molim vas hranila moj maca, on je siva.' He may have been choking, but I thought he said yes and I ended our conversation. I had just told him that I didn't give a fig for the house, and he was welcome to it but would he, please feed my poor little grey cat? I don't know if he did I like to think that someone took pity on poor Prince!

CHAPTER EIGHT

I often spoke to Rada in Osijek, and she hooted with laughter about us leaving in the middle of the night. 'You are both crazy nothing will happen to you! We are in Yugoslavia not Vietnam, come back and see me I miss you!' Sadly it would not be long before she discovered for herself that we were not crazy. Rada had a Croatian mother and a Serbian father, her husband was Croatian, and they had a little daughter called Daniela.

Towards the end of April that year, many friends of ours spoke in great anticipation of the forthcoming meeting they were organizing. It was to take place in Jagonjak with speakers from both Serbia and Baranja. Amongst whom would be Vojislav Sheshelj, the leader of SRS or Serbian Radical Party, who was coming to offer his support to the Serbians in Baranja, in attempting to keep Baranja out of the New Croatia. To become The Independent Republic of Serbian Krajina inside a federal Yugoslavia or to be part of Serbia. I didn't attend the meeting, but all the speakers made it clear that by whatever means necessary they would never become part of a Croatia that would forever regard them as second-class citizens. Historically and legally there was absolutely no case to argue that Baranja had ever been a part of Croatia, except for the redrawing of the borders by Tito, which had never been legally acknowledged or internationally recognised. After the meeting, the leaders of the Serb and Croatian communities met. Except for the Cheminac leaders, both sides agreed that if Yugoslavia collapsed and each country became a separate state, then Baranja would become part of Serbia.

The Serbs were the overwhelming majority in Baranja at this time. A previous census, falsified in Croatia, recorded all those that listed their ethnicity as Yugoslavian as being Croatian. Except for those living in Cheminac, the Croatians living in Baranja had not voted for the right-wing extremist parties but, for the moderate SDP or Social Democratic Party, the former communist party of Croatia. The Hungarian population largely ignored whatever was happening in the area outside their villages and seemed unconcerned by who was in power. Ilija and others had a meeting with Reihl-Kir the Osijek police chief (who had tried so hard to help us and others.) Chief Reihl-Kir asked that Croatian police officers would be allowed to control the meeting. The Serbs refused this request. However, they reached a compromise. They would film the meeting and give a copy to Chief Reihl-Kir, which he got. Coincidentally, it was this film, recorded by Ilija on our video camera, that I was shown by a prosecution barrister when I gave evidence at the Hague. They asked me about the meeting. It wasn't until I returned home and told Ilija about it that I learned that this was the film he had made!

I knew now that all the men in Jagonjak were arming themselves. Even though I was aware of it, I didn't believe that anything serious would happen. Many people had guns here, hunting rifles and handguns, no one seemed unduly concerned about their possession. Gun licences were relatively easy to obtain unless someone had a criminal record. Unless it was a hunting party, their guns weren't visible. With a turbulent history of invasion, by Romans, Turks, Hungarians, Austro-Hungarians and Hitlers army, people felt the need to protect themselves from possible invaders. In some areas of Yugoslavia, there were still wolves and black bears roaming freely, and the hunting of deer, boar and similar game for meat, was popular. There was a gun culture which made them feel they had a right to be armed. Now they went about their daily work as usual but, as the weeks passed there was a climate of fear and growing expectation that something dreadful was about to happen. I now made plans to return to England for a short visit to see my father. He had been in the hospital and was due home the 18th June. Also, the family wanted to organize a party for my mother's upcoming birthday on the 28th. I had arranged to fly to England on the 19th June, returning on the 1st July. However, two days before my planned departure I was awoken in the early hours of the morning 17th June to be given the dreadful news, that my father had died suddenly, in the hospital, a few hours earlier. Utterly devastated by the news, I flew back to England to be with the family in Coventry. We were so angry to discover that my father was subjected to a 'no resuscitation order' on his medical records, An order of which the family was unaware. Such practices nowadays have stopped, too late to help us or, my father. My mother had been waiting expectantly for his discharge later that same day, and the hospital failed to notify her in time for her to be at his side as he died. Married for 52 years, he had been her first and only sweetheart. Our utter devastation at his sudden death drove all thoughts of Baranja and Ilija from my mind. My mother was inconsolable and the weeks passed in something of a daze for me.

Then in late July 1991 I received a phone call from Rada in Osijek, she sounded very upset. Her husband had left her, and she and Daniela were staying at her mother's flat. I assumed it was a marital problem, not dreaming ethnicity was the issue. We talked, and she told me how she longed for the old days and was missing me, and I promised to call her soon. The very next day I got a call from a solicitor in Zagreb, Croatia. She told me that she was calling on behalf of Mrs. Hrastnic and if we wanted the deal with the house to continue then I should send fifteen hundred pounds to her, or we would lose the house. I said I would because I did expect to return. However, I told her that since I knew people living there, I would not pay either the telephone or electricity bills and held them responsible for their collection. They agreed to this, and I also asked if they could evict them from our property. They told me that they would try. I sent the money to the lawyer and heard nothing more. I never heard from them again and since neither of us wishes to set foot in Croatia, we never will. I left most of my household possessions when my first marriage ended. I certainly will never regret leaving bricks and mortar, and we have so much of which to be thankful. For Ilija and I survived this terrible time and went on to make a delightful, if somewhat unconventional home together, in the foothills of the mountains of Valjevo in Southern Serbia!

While I was in England, where we as a family were trying to come to terms with my father's loss, Ilija was going through his own, particular kind of hell in Jagonjak. I was extremely anxious about him we only managed to speak to each other a couple of times during July. But on each occasion, he told me not to return to Jagonjak yet because it was too dangerous to make the 34 km journey from Batina Bridge crossing to the village. In truth, I wasn't in any hurry to leave my mother, and we continued to comfort one another. We even began to decorate various rooms in our spacious home; I thought it may help her somehow.

After I had left, more and more people came flooding into Baranja from Croatia. Many were young men who were now taught to use the weapons that the Serbs had acquired. Attacks on Serbians living in Croatia, except for the Istrian area, that had begun in May 1990, escalated dramatically. By May 1991, widespread abuses and persecution of the Serbs were happening all across Croatia and Krajina. The barricades that the Serbs threw up all across Krajina was their only form of defence against Croatian paramilitary attacks on their towns and villages. From the beginning of May 1991 attacks by these Croatian forces were launched against many of the Serbian settlements in the area known as Eastern Serbian Krajina.

In later years, both the Croatian President Franjo Tudjman and Josip Boljkovac, who was his minister of internal affairs, admitted to an agenda. Which had been to initiate the fighting in Krajina (Baranja, East and West Slavonia, Srem, Banija, Kordun, Lika, and Northern Dalmatia). Paramilitary groups were ordered to attack the Serbs in those areas. The bigger plan was also to provoke a reaction from the Yugoslavian Army and draw them into the conflict. They were convinced that countries like Germany and indeed the Vatican, in support of this now staunchly, Catholic state would have an excuse to recognize Croatia as an independent state. And that the World would see Croatia as a victim, rather than as the aggressor.

Ironically the commanding generals of the Yugoslavian Army, Navy and Airforce were all Croatian. In their naivety, the Serbians of Krajina had absolutely no idea of this greater plan. If Tudjman had not begun his assault on the Serbians living in Krajina, there might never have been a civil war. The Serbians simple wish was to remain inside a Federal Yugoslavia while Tudjman and his cronies dreamed of re-establishing the first Independent State of Croatia, which Hitler had allowed them set up.

Before 1941, Croatia had never been an independent state or country. Instead, they had been the vassals of, in their turn, the Romans, Hungarians, Austro-Hungarians until finally becoming a part of Yugoslavia. The much-maligned Serbian President Slobodan Milosevic desperately tried to keep the federation together. His last attempt was to offer a confederation to the former federal republics, comprising independent countries. He believed that it would be impossible for these independent states to be able to support viable economies alone. In its heyday, before its destruction, Yugoslavia had been a leading force in the non-aligned movement of countries which, after being established 1961, at one period, represented more than 50% of the World's population. Made up of those leaders of developing countries who advocated a middle course between the major powers of the West and Eastern Bloc, the removal of Yugoslavia from this sphere certainly weakened the organisation.

In Jagonjak, sniper fire had killed several people in and around the village. The men were manning the barricades, but supplies were still coming in, and the people began to hoard whatever they could uncertain of their future. During daylight hours, life was relatively normal even the schools were open. However, during the hours of darkness, families cowered in their homes behind the barricades, waiting for the attacks they thought were inevitable and wondering if they should leave their farms and escape to Serbia. Eventually, life became so dangerous in Jagonjak in May 1991 that before I left, I witnessed all the young mothers with their children, boarding the buses that would evacuate them to Serbia. Along with the women and children from the other villages in Baranja. Kind families in Serbian towns like Prigrevica welcomed them into their homes. The majority of those living in Baranja at this time and probably throughout the rest of Krajina still hoped vainly to carry on living as peacefully as before, and they fully expected the Yugoslavian Army to restore order. That the whole country would return to normality because Yugoslavia still existed and Croatia was still part of this federation. Their paramilitary groups were illegal forces acting outside the laws under the Yugoslavian constitution.

The ethnic Serbians of Croatia and Krajina were totally unaware of the might of the Western propaganda forces ranged against them at this time. They had lost the propaganda war before they ever realized they were in a fight. Croatia and Slovenia declared independence on 25th June 1991. But this was very early days, and many refused to believe that it would actually, happen. In fact, neither state was recognized internationally until 1992. The ordinary soldiers of the Yugoslavian army at this time were all young conscripts doing their compulsory national service. It had always been the policy of the army not to allow the conscripts to serve their term in their own, federal state. Therefore, when Slovenia and Croatia declared their independence many of these young 18 to 21-year-old conscripts from other federal states were trapped in their barracks. Eventually, their release was negotiated, but they had to leave all their weapons and equipment behind. In what was later described by Slovenia and Croatia as their heroic war against the Yugoslavian Army, some of the young conscripts were killed. One such killing was captured by a television news service. As a Yugoslavian Army (J.N.A) armoured vehicle was being driven out of their barracks in Split, Croatia, a crowd of local men climbed onto the vehicle. They opened the hatch and dragged out a 19- year- old Macedonian Yugoslavian Army conscript. Graphic television coverage showed one of the mob, twisting and breaking the young man's neck. The crowd bayed and screamed and when the murderer was sure that his victim was dead he threw his body back through the hatch of the vehicle. The young conscripts of the J.N.A were not only, not professional soldiers but also, were under orders not to open fire and had little or no ammunition. It was no glorious victory. But it was another glorious victory of the propaganda machinery being so expertly manipulated by Croatia and her Allies.

I heard about the conscripts from some of their mothers, fathers, and grandparents who always wanted to tell me about their sons and grandsons. When these young men were called up to do their national service, their family arranged an enormous send-off for them. They invited most of their neighbours for this was seen as a right of passage or, his coming of age. Ilija and I attended many of them. It was a point of pride for these youngsters to serve their country, even though army life was hard. It is also important to remember that many of these young men that were serving in Croatia and Slovenia were from distant federations, like Macedonia, Montenegro, Bosnia. They were killed far from home and had no idea why they were being treated as the enemy.

By June 1991, Tudjman had made his move against Baranja. In the town of Beli Manastir, which was controlled by the Croats and was the administrative centre for Baranja, all ethnic Serbs had been dismissed from the civilian police force. The paramilitary wings of the political parties like HDZ from Croatia and armed with assault rifles were stationed at the police station along with the regular police force. The local government, schools, and local medical centres had also been ethnically cleansed of Serbian employees. The elderly residents of the only old people's home in Baranja were unceremoniously moved out, and the Croatian paramilitaries moved in to take it over to use for their accommodation facilities.

From early October 1990, Ilija and the representatives from all the villages in Baranja had been holding regular secret meetings at the homes of friends to discuss what was rapidly becoming a worsening situation. Other Serbs had tried through political means to negotiate with the Croats by peaceful means, with written protests regarding the loss of employment in the town of all Serbs. They made representations at local and national levels with the HDZ. However, it became increasingly apparent, with the HDZ slogan of Croatia for Croatians that they had absolutely no interest in reaching any compromise with the Serbian population. Their stance was that Serbs must accept, unconditionally all the new policies of the latest Croatian constitution. Or, face the consequences. These veiled threats, from a nation which had committed acts of genocide against the Serbs, Jews, and Roma within living memory of many of its citizens, were impossible to ignore.

And people began to disappear. The paramilitary police of the right-wing political parties, under the direction of their leaders, entered the homes of Serbs and dissident Croatians and took men away. One of the leaders of the Serbian Democratic Party in Virovitica, a town East of Zagreb was arrested, tortured and shot in the back of the neck by the local police. He survived and finally escaped. Eventually, he found me in Baranja asking me to write down his story and try to get justice for him. I wrote his story and included all the hospital reports and affidavits he provided, but I still failed to get justice for him. In the town of Sisak, situated South of Zagreb, over 600 villagers were massacred. There are many more instances of the summary executions of Serbian families. Some are recorded because family members survived to tell of their experiences. In the coastal city of Split three, brave, Croatian policemen were so appalled by the tortures used on Serbian prisoners in Split prison, that they decided to go together to Zagreb. Here they tried to protest to President Tudjman in person. On the return journey, they were ambushed but, fortunately, survived the attempted assassinations.

One Serbian woman, searching for her missing husband and two sons aged 21 and 23, had been to the Osijek Police Headquarters day after day, asking why they had been arrested. Finally, she was told by a police officer, who was later indicted for war crimes, to 'check with the pathology department.' Then, 'they are dead,' it would be better if she now kept quiet. The arrest and disappearance of Serbs and other opponents of the regime were now happening on a daily basis throughout Croatia. During and after the conflict the majority of the murders and torturing of innocent civilians went unpunished. After a few show trials, the cases were quietly dropped or the criminals were granted an amnesty. Even as late as 2015 there are still valiant attempts by some to bring these perpetrators of such evil to trial. But, with the extremist H.D.Z party back in power, it is doubtful that even the European Union can exert sufficient pressure on Croatia to punish anyone.

There were just 19 of them who met at a friend's house in Beli Manastir on the night of 18th August 1991. Ordinary young men, not all were ethnic Serbs, there was a Muslim, a Czech and several of mixed Serbian/Croatian ethnicity, but all shared one goal. To keep Baranja part of a united Yugoslavia. They, with the others who heard the intense firefight and ran to help them, liberated Beli Manastir and eventually all Baranja. They fought against enormous odds and some were to die or were wounded. All were to eventually be driven from their family homes and land. Had Serbia been victorious in their fight against Croatia then no doubt these men would have been lauded as heroes. Instead of which they all are ignored and the graves of those who were killed largely left untended.

Before this meeting on the night of the 18TH August to discuss the situation, it was not only the Serbian villages in Baranja that had been barricaded. For now the Serbian residents in the towns and larger villages of rest of Krajina, also erected barricades to defend the Serbian areas. Having had enough of the attacks by the Blackshirts of the Croatian paramilitary forces, they saw no other recourse. They feared a massacre because despite repeated pleas for help the Yugoslav Army had not come to aid them.

The night of the 18th, Ilija and his fellow men from Jagonjak and some surrounding villages made their way through the forest to Beli Manastir, avoiding the Croatian paramilitary patrols and met the other eleven of their group in a friend's home. Ironically, given what was to happen during this coming night, Ilija's mother had brought him a large, freshly baked bread earlier that evening. She said 'My dear son, tomorrow is a Holy day, please do not do anything other than stay in bed until late and then read one of your books and don't forget to pray.' Ilija didn't remain in bed until late or, read a book, but he certainly prayed.

After their meeting, the men volunteered to relieve the local Serbs manning the barricade protecting a Serbian area in this part of the town of Beli Manastir. The barricade was down by the railway tracks. About 2 a.m. in the morning, they saw several dozen Croatian Special Policemen carrying their assault rifles advancing on their barricade. The men later learned that a neighbour had alerted these police to their presence in the home of their friend. A firefight began and Ilija and the other men joined the barricade to return fire. Now, as police reinforcements were rushed to the area, Serbs and others, from other parts of the town joined in the fight. As the fighting erupted, the Yugoslavian army soldiers remained in their barracks on the outskirts of Beli Manastir. Their policy was to wait until daylight to see if they could intervene. Meanwhile, reports came that as the Serbs drove the Croatian militia back, Branimir Glavas, who had come to oversee the Croatian forces, escaped in an ambulance. He had sought shelter in the Yugoslavian Army barracks from where they took him back to Osijek.

In the confusion and firing, there were tragedies on both sides. The Croats had casualties, killed and wounded in the fighting. The first to die amongst the Serbs was the son of one of our friends. However, there were far fewer casualties amongst the Serbs than the Croats. One of the young Serb fighters who became isolated and was under fire all night from snipers as he sought cover behind an oak tree had, by morning, completely lost his mind. His friends disarmed him and some of the people took him into their home to try and calm him but he just screamed incessantly. He was a good friend of ours and sadly never recovered spending many years in hospitals. The people of the town told of how they lay on the floor of their houses all that day and night. At 6 am, the Yugoslav Army was seen on the streets with a tank and armoured personnel carriers. They drove around observing and as they appeared the streetfighting stopped, then, as they drove away it resumed. Incredibly, Ilija climbed to the very top of one of the enormous silo's at the town's flour mill and hung a Serbian flag from the top. As soon as he descended, he was promptly arrested by a Yugoslavian army officer. 'Please Ilija,' he said, 'we can not take sides in this matter, you must remove the flag!' Ilija said he wouldn't. The officer replied that he couldn't be bothered to climb all the way up to do it and Ilija was released.

The Croatian police were steadily being driven back to their headquarters in the centre of the town. At 11.am, there was a cease-fire arranged and both sides collected their dead and wounded. The Croatian forces then appealed to the Yugoslav Army for help in evacuating their men to Osijek. But, by an alternative route because they claimed that informers had warned them that the villagers from Jagonjak and Bolman were to mount an ambush if they tried to go via the main route to Osijek. The local commander of the Yugoslavian army telephoned Ilija's group and told them of the Croatian plea. And said that the ceasefire would be extended until 3.pm that afternoon. The Serbs did not trust the Croats but, because the army was arranging it, they agreed to the withdrawal. A large convoy comprising Croatian Special Police, ordinary police, and those civilians from Beli Manastir and the surrounding villages, who wanted to leave with them, was organized. The army escorted them as far as Baranski Petrovo Selo where they crossed the River Drava using large flat-bottomed boats supplied by Croatia.

At 3 pm, that afternoon, Ilija and the fighters entered the abandoned police headquarters. They triumphantly took down the Croatian flag and raised a Serbian one. Ilija then rang me in England to tell me what had happened and to reassure me as much as he could that he was alright and safe. That night, however, Croatians from the villages of Cheminac, Kozarac and Petlovac tried to recapture Beli Manastir. While Serbian villagers from Jagonjak, Bolman, Karanac and Knezevi Vinogradi came to reinforce the Serbian fighters in Beli Manastir. Street battles raged for the next two days and nights until the Croats finally withdrew to their fortified positions outside the town of Darda. Ilija and others now began to check the Croatian areas of Beli Manastir, street by street and house by house. The remaining Croatian fighters now surrendered and it soon became evident that the town was almost deserted. Of the 23,000 inhabitants, very few civilians remained.

One of those that did was my kum Dushanka and her husband. She told me later how she and her husband had spent several nights on the floor, under blankets, hidden behind their couch. When she heard the sound of boots entering her house, she was terrified of who she would see standing there in her sitting-room. Would it be Croatians or Serbs? Both she and her husband had for some time been unable to leave their home for fear of being vilified by Croatian neighbours who had shouted insults at them, asking them why they were still there. These were neighbours that they had lived alongside for the previous twenty or so years. This madness, as she called it, had never happened before Franjo Tudjman began his campaign of hate against the Serbs. Fight or flight had been the only option for the Serbs.

The Serbian fighters were now organized into a rapid response force, given blue uniforms to wear and appointed as police Special Forces. The police headquarters was their base and they were under the control of the Police Chief in Beli Manastir. They attempted to establish law and order again because now into the deserted town came the opportunist criminals. A call was made to their base to report that groups of men were attempting to steal the lorries from Grada, a local building supply company. They arrived there to find some civilians who claimed they had an official order to confiscate the lorries. Asked to produce the order they couldn't. They were arrested, taken to the Police H.Q and subsequently released. The Yugoslavian army at this time remained inside their barracks and flatly refused to have anything to do with the conflict. They repeatedly said that they couldn't take sides and were now under strict orders to stay inside their barracks.

Meanwhile, around the 21st August Ilija was able to visit his mother and our home in Jagonjak, managing to find one of our cats which he brought to Beli Manastir. To his relief, the village was unscathed and people were going about their daily work without constant fear of attack by snipers or shelling. On the other hand, when he went to Cheminac to check on Franjo and his sister Maria, of the village of two or three thousand souls, barely thirty or so remained. The others having left for Croatia. Ilija had been fearful that some of the Croatian extremists living in Cheminac would take revenge on his sister, a Serb and her husband a Croat, who had protected some Serbians in the village. In the event, they were perfectly alright, although extremely shocked by the events of the previous weeks.

On Ilija's return to Beli Manastir, further evidence of this unfolding tragedy was evident. Streets, empty of children, shoppers and others, going about their daily business, was a stark reminder that something dreadful had happened. Ilija found it incredible that people who had lived in relative harmony from the time of the national reconciliation after the 2nd World War could suddenly be persuaded to hate each other. Even more incredible to think that after all they had suffered in Croatia during that war that Serbs again had to fight for their very survival. He had gone to school in this community, fallen in love in this community and his friends were of this community. Now, he didn't know where many of them were, or even if they were alive. He and other members of their defence force now toured the streets using megaphones urging people to stay calm and not to fire any guns otherwise they stood the risk of being shot at by their patrols. He was able to telephone me quite often during these few days and I soon sensed how upset he was.

He and the other fighters had only ever intended to stop the terror being visited on Serbs and Roma by the paramilitary forces of Tudjman's extremist political party. Their fight had never been against the Yugoslavian people who had listed themselves as Croatian. They now searched for the radio equipment which had been taken and hidden in a nearby village. It was reinstalled and broadcasts began from the local radio station, urging people to stay calm and not to panic. Now came a time of confusion. Those that could not be fighters either because of their age or they wouldn't volunteer began to form an ad hoc police force, instead of joining the Special Forces. They now tried hard to restore order in the town. For the first few months, everyone was paid by coupons which could be redeemed for basic food items. The people of the town were heavily dependent on their relatives in the villages for cheese, egg, poultry, milk, and pork in addition to all the vegetables and fruit they produced.

This was a time of great heroism by some. Others took to looting Beli Manastir and committing acts of murderous savagery. The two must never be linked. Those that fought for their belief that they could never live as second -class citizens inside Tudjman's new Croatia. For they were not just ethnic Serbs, but Roma, Czech, Serb/Croats, Serb/Hungarians, Croat/Hungarians, or Croats but, were, in fact, Yugoslavians. Some fought for the glory of Ancient Serbia, others for Yugoslavia. The murderous bands of criminal opportunists who arrived in Baranja now, or, some local men who joined them, should in the opinion of many, be regarded as being men without nationality. They had their own agenda for coming out of the shadows to commit their crimes as the local defence force continued to fight to free Baranja of the terror visited upon them by Tudjman.

Late in the evening of 27th of August fighting erupted around the village of Darda, fierce fighting continued until the 28th and there were heavy casualties on both sides. Eventually, the Croats withdrew through Mece and then Bilje. Finally, they retreated across the bridge over the River Drava to Osijek. The bridge was then destroyed by order of Branimir Glavas, now the Chief of Police in Osijek following the murder of Chief Rehl-Kir.

The Yugoslavian Army brought trucks to the battle area and took away both Serbian and Croatian dead and wounded. They were all taken across Batina Bridge, to Sombor Hospital in Serbia. The Croatians were then exchanged for Serbian prisoners. There were no medicines at all at this time at the medical centre in Beli Manastir. Baranja did not have a hospital. There was now a lull in the fighting but, within days, the Croatians began the indiscriminate shelling of Baranja. Villages like Jagonjak were shelled where there were no targets that could conceivably be described as military ones. The centre of Beli Manastir was also being hit especially around the piazza, the flour mill, and waterworks which were amongst those regularly targeted.

Ilija and the special forces now returned on the 3rd September from the Bilje frontline to find a very different Beli Manastir to the one they had left. The large supermarket in the centre of the town had been looted and lay empty and deserted. Televisions, entertainment centres, domestic appliances, household goods, everything one may find in a large supermarket had disappeared. The next discovery was the open and empty vaults of all the town banks. Now, down by the railroad tracks, where the first fighting had begun some two weeks previously, the railway sheds were empty. All the goods in transit to Hungary, including hundreds of generators, cultivators, photocopiers, an enormous consignment of Nike trainers and pallets of bonded goods, like whiskey, brandy and perfumes were gone. There were 14 freight cars which had been loaded with sugar and were now empty. But, the greatest thefts of all, were those of the oil and petrol reserves from the biggest garages and storage tanks in the area. This left Baranja seriously short of fuel. Ilija and others tried to investigate what had happened in their absence. Since there was only one way in and out of Baranja by road and this was under the control of the Serbs, everything must have been moved across the bridge at Batina into Serbia. They now discovered that convoys of tankers and trucks had been seen crossing this bridge. From the information gathered they knew that the brother of the man who was soon to become the police chief at Darda, a man called Kostich, had organised the thefts.

This same Kostich had appeared at the Police headquarters in Beli Manastir on the 20th August claiming that he was under orders from President Milosevic to take over the town and organize the police force. He had been given short shrift by the special forces who regarded him as an ordinary criminal. He was a former police chief in Darda in the mid-1980's and had been dismissed from this post after charges of customs and taxation fraud were levelled against him. He disappeared following his arrest and no one was sure what had become of him. He couldn't produce any signed authority from the office of the Serbian President Milosevic. This claim became something of a joke amongst the special forces and regular police service. For the corrupt Army and militia officers, who now seemed to flood into

Baranja from Serbia, all claimed that they had the authorization of President Milosevic. This authorization, they assumed, would allow them to remove or confiscate hundreds of cars, machinery and plant from the factories and companies of Baranja. In some cases, they were successful and hundreds of cars, lorries, plant and machinery disappeared from the premises of the Remont Company. This company had become a virtual warehouse stocked with not only new cars but also those confiscated, quite illegally, from Croatians. Much of the criminals looted plunder was initially taken there before transiting to Serbia. Where the Baranja police Special Forces could prevent the thefts, they did. But sometimes, as in the case of the Remont company, the J.N.A were in control of the site. Therefore, nothing could be done. No one ever produced any signed order from President Milosevic authorizing such removals or confiscations.

This is not to say that all the crimes were committed by people outside of Baranja. There were some from the ad hoc police forces and even some of the Special Forces who took revenge on Croatian prisoners. Two buses were loaded with prisoners from the Beli Manastir police headquarters and driven out of Baranja during the last week of August 1991. Ilija told me that just before they left for the battle at Darda, he was standing outside the police headquarters and saw the two buses loaded with people. He asked the driver who was wearing some sort of uniform, but not army or police, what was happening. The man told him that they were taking the prisoners to Dalj, on the right bank of the River Danube in Slavonije, for a prisoner exchange. Ilija didn't have a chance to see who was on the buses. When Ilija returned to Beli Manastir on the 3rd September, Ruza, an old school friend of his, asked him to try and find her father, who was Hungarian. He was one of those who had been imprisoned in the police station and taken away on one of the buses. Ilija sought out the driver and asked him where they had taken the people on the buses. He shrugged and told Ilija that they were exchanged as he had said before. Ilija went and told Ruza, but she said despite all her attempts to find out, no one knew anything about a prisoner exchange taking place involving her father. Ilija again tried to trace him but was met with shrugs and denials.To our best knowledge, Ruza's father, nor any other of the men who had been taken away on the buses, were ever seen again.

There is a saying that when a ship sinks, 'shit' is one of the first things to float. This was certainly true in Baranja. For while the battles were being fought to secure the borders the carpetbaggers moved in. These people now assumed the role of local lawmakers and enacted some shameful laws. One such law was that Croatians and every member of their family would lose their jobs because their presence was not conducive to a healthy working atmosphere and would upset other workers. Other such idiotic, cruel and unjust laws were also enacted by these 'Serbian Patriots' not so patriotic they wanted to fight for what they believed in. They sought the vestiges of power. Their next pronouncement was that anyone who didn't return to live in Baranja by a specified date in October would never be allowed to return. A pretty stupid condition aimed at the Croatians who had fled, but there were thousands of Serbians who had also left during the fighting. Both these new laws were to punish many who had never been a part of the HDZ and its right-wing anti-Serbian policies. They were now trying to introduce ethnically based conditions when some good friends of ours, who were Croatian, fought with the Territorials and later joined the Army Pioneers to defend Baranja. The actions of these few unimportant individuals did not in any way reflect what most people in Baranja wanted or thought.

During the week before the battle at Darda, several incidents occurred at the Police headquarters in Beli Manastir that revolted and infuriated Ilija. On one occasion, he heard someone screaming from one of the interview rooms and went in there to find a young priest being beaten by a local policeman. This man, a former postman turned policeman was a sadist and Ilija, pushing him aside took the young priest, Milich, outside to his car. Ilija told him not to be afraid and that he would take him home, which he did. When they arrived at his home in the town, he found a mother and father with six other children. When they saw Ilija in his uniform, they were terrified.

Milich calmed them and explained how Ilija had helped him. Now Ilija also assisted the family by finding food for them, for the father and mother had been victims of this new law and lost their jobs at the milk processing plant. Several days later Milich approached Ilija and asked him if he could help him leave Baranja because he wanted to continue his theological studies at Djakovo Seminary in Croatia. Ilija took him to Serbia and then to the Hungarian border at Backi Breg and gave him a small sum of money to help him get to Croatia. Later, Milich's family all left for Croatia.

Ilija tried to help others who were being held at the Police station. Eight people in one cell, one of whom was Dusan Jakshic, from Dubosevica, were released before the end of 1991. And by the end of January 1992, all remaining prisoners had been released. Some returned to their villages some went to Croatia. Most of these prisoners had been active members of the HDZ and all those linked to the HDZ had been arrested and investigated during the previous August or September. The real extremists, responsible for the attacks on Serbs, had left for Croatia with the Croatian paramilitaries. Ilija took me to meet Dusan Jakshic at his home in the Duboshevica in late 1992 after the UN had taken charge of the area and all the special forces had been disarmed and decommissioned. They embraced each other warmly and the man gestured to me by moving his hands from his heart towards Ilija. They were both quite emotional and then another man joined us, neither of us recalls his name. He was a school teacher and had been imprisoned with Dusan and we took photographs of everyone. As we were drinking coffee with the Jakshic family, from a cupboard he brought about thirty empty cigarette packets. Ilija laughed in amazement and told me that he had often bought the prisoner's cigarettes and that Dusan had kept all the empty packets. It was very touching and felt very proud of Ilija. At the same time, I wondered why such a nice ordinary man as Dusan had been subjected to such imprisonment. But at least, Ilija had ensured that they were not ill-treated all the time he was on duty at the Police headquarters. When I asked others why they had treated prisoners the way some of them did, their reply was that the Croats treated their Serb prisoners much worse than that and frequently murdered them. Revenge was a motive I heard a lot of people claim. Sometimes, from refugees who had indeed suffered terribly at the hands of the Croats. Sometimes from others who had not. Understandable as their feeling may have been, it did not make it any less horrifying or justifiable.

CHAPTER NINE

In the early morning of 7ᵗʰ October 1991, Ilija and 4 other members of the special forces were on patrol between checkpoints on the banks of the River Drava. Suddenly they came under fire and their jeep was hit by a burst of 20mm machine gun fire from across the River on the Croatian side. As their driver swerved along the top of the embankment trying to evade the fire, the jeep was hit and it careered downwards, overturning and rolling several times. It ended up on its side. Three of the men were thrown out, but Ilija and Nebojsha (Fritz, who later proved to be such a steadfast friend to us) were still inside. Fritz climbed out, but Ilija found that he couldn't and as the men began to pull him free he began to scream. He had broken his right shoulder blade, ribs and torn the muscles in his chest. Another of their patrol jeeps came and recovered Ilija and drove him across Batina Bridge to Sombor Hospital in Serbia. The hospital was full of the wounded from the battles now raging around Vukovar. Because they were inundated with so many urgent cases as soon as the doctor had strapped Ilija's right side and fitted a sling, Ilija asked to be taken back to Beli Manastir.

A journalist from the Serbian newspaper Politika Jovan D. had been in Beli Manastir covering the war since around the 21ˢᵗ of August he heard that Ilija had been wounded and came to visit him. Ilija gave him my telephone number in England and he rang me some days later. In a town with only a few hours of electricity a week and one working, outside line, this was no mean feat. I understood the gist of what he was saying but with his pigeon English and my pigeon

Serbian I couldn't ascertain the seriousness of his injuries. I took the earliest flight that I could from Heathrow to Serbia and Jovan met me at the airport. He was a slight figure, middle-aged, with a kind face and he was now able to make me understand that Ilija had been discharged from the hospital. Naturally, I felt enormously relieved, almost elated, as we set off for his home in Vrsac on the Romanian border with Serbia. This was his hometown and he explained that he had to make some arrangements before we could travel to Baranja, some 300 km distant.

The journey to Vrsac took about one and half hours and we arrived just in time for supper! The family was very kind but after we had eaten, I suddenly felt exhausted and was shown into their guest room. They let me sleep late into the morning because Jovan had gone to make the arrangements for our journey. They had formed a relief committee in the town and were collecting money for the refugees who were flooding into Serbia from Krajina. Many were arriving with just the clothes they wore, having had no time to pack any belongings. Their plight was pitiful and so I donated 1,000 Deutsch mark to their fund. Jovan had refused to accept any money from me for his expenses and I felt a donation on his behalf would repay him a little. In the event when his next article appeared in Politika he mentioned the contribution and attributed it to me.

We set off very early for our trip to Baranja because we had to arrive and cross the Bridge at Batina before the curfew at 8 pm. The journey took us around 5 hours and we crossed the bridge in the early afternoon without any difficulty. I had no idea where Ilija was since he had left our home in Jagonjak. All the members of his group of special forces were allocated houses in some abandoned properties in Beli Manastir. Most of their owners had fled to Osijek and when the refugees arrived from Krajina, they were rehoused in them. The Red Cross moved most of the electrical appliances like fridges, freezers, cookers, etc. and beds, chairs tables and sofas, from the empty houses. They were then sent to a storage area to prevent them being looted and later redistributed to the refugees many of whom arrived with nothing more than a few plastic bags. They mostly felt nothing regarding the fact that they were in someone else's home. This was the harsh reality, people were trying to survive. Many of them had nothing to return to in Croatian because they houses were burned or blown up. Entire villages had been destroyed. Jovan took me to the house where Ilija was staying and we were overjoyed to see each other. His right side was heavily strapped from shoulder to waist and he was extremely pale and much thinner than when I had left but at least, he was alive and safe for the moment. He had managed to bring a few of our possessions from Jagonjak including our clothes and promised as soon as ever it was feasible, to fetch the remaining, bigger items. It wasn't comfortable, but it was adequate and, fortunately, I had all my winter clothing including a ski suit which was to prove invaluable. Jovan said his goodbyes and left for Vrsac the next day.

That evening at around 8.pm the shelling that Ilija had warned me about began. My first reaction was to go and look out of the window as I heard the first whoosh and then an explosion. Ilija's first reaction was to shout at me and go into full army mode. 'Open the windows' (to prevent the glass shattering if the air pressure rose caused by shells falling close to the house). He now grabbed me and hurried me outside. 'Now listen and count, when the shell lands we usually have about 20 seconds to get to next door's basement' he said, as a company sergeant-major might, by shouting orders in my ear. We began to run and then there was another whoosh and suddenly I found myself flat on my back. Ilija had pushed me down as the shell was heading in our direction. As he did the butt of his Kalashnikov gun, hit me on the head. I thought, never mind the artillery killing me another hit like that could! He said 'Jump up and run as soon as I tell you.' There was a loud bang as the shell landed on a nearby street and then we both got up and hurried to the basement of the neighbour's house some 20m away. To arrive in a situation like that from relative normality is the strangest sensation.

It was frightening, yet it didn't seem real. It was as if Ilija were ridiculously overacting in some amateur dramatics production. Then as I watched from the doorway of the basement, I saw Ilija running to another neighbours house, the home of an elderly couple. Ilija reappeared with a white-haired lady and she was holding his arm. As they stumbled towards me, I could hear her sobbing and then the full horror of that moment hit me. Her husband was bedridden and refused to leave his bed and take shelter. Gradually over the next weeks, it became must worse and eventually he allowed Ilija to carry him to the shelter. Ilija somehow managed to do this despite the fact that his collar bone was not healing properly and he was always in tremendous pain at times for many years to come. That first night I witnessed the other neighbours without secure basements begin arriving. The basement we entered had large double doors and was usually used as a garage. It was enormous and had obviously been used many times in its capacity as a shelter because there were chairs and blankets, candles and bottles of water which people had left there. Ilija and all the other men who had brought their families to the shelter now left to go to the front lines in case the shelling heralded a ground attack. Ilija couldn't go on patrols because of his inability to carry his gun, but he would be with his men as much as he could. All the women and children were now alone at night. The older men, anyone who was fit enough to walk, had already gone before darkness fell, to guard the waterworks in the fields outside the town. Seeing these old timers form up and march off was for me very touching. They even kept in step as they set off with their old rifles held proudly on their shoulders. Sometimes, if one got out of step, the others shot them such looks of disgust it was necessary to stifle a giggle.

Our house was cold and miserable. Without any of Ilija's family close by and before, I made some friends, I felt as if I had arrived in hell. I now kept my ski suit by the side of the bed so that I could immediately put it on at the sound of the first explosion and then make my way to the shelter. There was rarely any electricity and when it was turned on there was never enough wattage to use an electric cooker or even the TV. Our last remaining cat, ladybird or Bubica as Ilija called her, now disappeared. I was very sad, she had been such a character and absolutely adored Ilija. He had rescued her from an Osijek street as a little kitten and they had a special bond. Once Ilija had been part of an afternoon patrol, at the beginning of the attacks on Jagonjak, searching for a sniper who was firing into the village. He had been crawling on his stomach through the tall grass in the fields around trying to reach the tree-line when suddenly Bubica found him and began to rub her head all over his face. She then climbed onto his back before returning to rub and lick his face until finally he reached his goal. It had been far too dangerous to raise his head and they had been trying hard to move without being seen and it would be an understatement to say that her attentions were very unwelcome. I never learnt the details of what the other members of the patrol said to him after they failed to find the sniper. He apparently had disappeared and so Ilija picked up Bubica put her into his backpack and took her home.

The plight of all the animals during conflicts is sometimes overlooked. Some people who had gone to Osijek left their dogs chained in their yards. In the villages, livestock had been abandoned without food or water. One of the more enterprising of the carpetbaggers organized a fellow group of entrepreneurs to remove all the animals from the abandoned farms. Some were slaughtered and loaded into refrigerated lorries, others were taken across Batina Bridge to Serbia where they were sold. There was no doubt at all that the action was necessary there was no one to care for these animals. However, while many people in Baranja especially the refugees were short of food a valuable source of meat and dairy produce disappeared into Serbia making the perpetrators very wealthy.

Ilija recovered well enough to go back to active duties by the end of October. However, his shoulder blade never healed properly and left him with a permanently weakened and sometimes painful right arm and shoulder. He was awarded a pension, but this never materialized either then or now. His involvement in the defence of Baranja meant that he was either on duty patrolling the front lines or, part of excursions deep into Croatia. Their remit was to check on what, if any, military build-ups were underway. Even when he came home, many of the unmarried members of his group came with him and they would spend the next few hours discussing what they had been doing, seen or felt. They had already been debriefed at their headquarters, this was their way of relaxing. I hated it. During one of these visits, one of the group walked into the kitchen and opened the fridge. Now he guffawed and loudly exclaimed to the others, what sort of fighting man had all this salad crap in his fridge? Where was the beer? Although he later denied it, I think I offended Ilija's male sensibilities when, after this inspection of my fridge I ordered this rowdy bunch out and told them not to come back. I understood that they were stressed and were just trying to relax, but I found it increasingly difficult to cope with this sort of life. When we did manage to watch the news on TV everyone was outraged by the bias and innuendo of the reporting. Croatia was the innocent party, had been attacked without any provocation and Serbs were murdering all Croats in their beds. Ilija knew that I was unhappy, unable to cope with the nightly shelling, cold, lack of electricity and ultimately my isolation without friends or family support. Finally, in the middle of November, he suggested that I return to England and try to counter some of the negative news reports, many of which were not just unfounded they were downright lies! We agreed that there was little I could do to contribute in Beli Manastir.

Ilija drove me to Belgrade airport on the 16th November 1991. The flight was early the next morning and so we decided to book into the Hyatt Regency Hotel to enjoy a night of luxury for a change. At least a hot bath and a good meal and a few special hours alone together. Baranja was dark and cold in the evenings and as we drove into the brilliantly lit capital city of Belgrade, we both felt some anger. Life was going on as if nothing were happening. We hadn't expected sackcloth and ashes, in fact, I am not sure what we expected. Probably not normality and indifference. The Hyatt lived up to its price tag and reputation and we dined well, took an inordinately long bath together and just for the evening tried to forget all about war and sadness. I made a quick trip down to the duty-free shop in the hotel basement and bought Ilija some Yves St Laurant cologne. I wanted to spoil him. He was fiercely committed to his beliefs and often took unnecessary risks on patrols. Some of his men had told me how he would carry a camera and in the middle of the fighting would jump up and take a photograph. Another quirk of his was to always be immaculately turned out when reporting for duty. This included his trademark cologne which his friends said would waft into the room before he ever appeared. It used to make me giggle to watch one man, in particular, become furiously angry because when he came to collect Ilija for duty Ilija would dash off to get a quick splash of cologne and keep him waiting. Not nice but funny! And had earned him the reputation of being 'nuts'. This and a few other little traits of his, such as the way he had fearlessly confronted Kostich and others like him ensured he was given a wide berth and show a healthy respect by others.

He and I were almost, but not quite, to the point of no return. It was probably very selfish of me, but I hated feeling second best to his war. At this time, I didn't feel it had much to do with me only that I cared about the people I knew who were embroiled in it. But I didn't feel any commitment to them and if I were to do what Ilija had asked it would be for him, no one else. There was nothing about this man that I didn't like and much that I did. He was inordinately kind, a rescuer of any homeless person (as he then and always has since referred to the stray animals he has rescued.) A passionate lover, I always longed for the nights when he would slip into bed and wrap himself around me. We had not lost our passion for each other but sometimes when he did have 24 hrs leave he was so exhausted he immediately fell asleep. As we kissed goodbye at the departure gate half of me wondered if we would ever be together again. We made the usual promises as one does at such times and after a final embrace, he walked away and I turned into the departure lounge.

It is probably normal that in times of great stress and confusion that the mind finds a way to help the body survive. Jude had driven my Mum to the airport and I was so happy to see their smiling faces and be enfolded in their arms. As we walked towards the car park, a passing vehicle backfired and I immediately put my hands over my head and knelt down. Jude and Mum looked at me in astonishment and I laughed saying I thought I had dropped something. Jude knew but helped me cover up the reaction from my Mum. If you have been in a war zone, your reaction to loud bangs is instinctive and completely beyond your control. A similar thing happened a few days later when Mum and I were on the doorstep waving goodbye to some friends. Mum's next door neighbour slammed her front door shut and I again immediately knelt down and covered my head with my arms. This time, Mum held me close as I stood up. 'I don't want you to go back there again' She said. 'You look so thin and pale, I have never seen you like this before.' I tried to contact Ilija over the next few days to make sure he was alright, but the single telephone line into the police headquarters was always busy. I worried about him constantly and now began watching and reading news reports in the British media about the situation in Baranja. Most of these reports were so biased and being made by reporters who obviously had never been there. They absolutely infuriated me. They even had a special way of reporting incursions and attacks. For instance 'unknown persons attacked the village of ... during the night and there were reports of several casualties amongst the non-combatants living there. This meant that Croatian forces had attacked a village and killed civilians living there. Whereas, Serbian extremists attacked a village in........ possibly wounding and killing, without pity, utterly defenceless women, children and elderly people. These are not the exact reports I heard, but similar in design and motive.

I now began to call and write to British newspapers and one afternoon I telephoned the B.B.C News in London. I asked to speak to their duty news editor regarding reports that were being made on the B.B.C. News. I was connected to someone who said he spoke on behalf of the editor and asked me what I wanted. After introducing myself, I explained to him about living in Osijek, fleeing to Baranja and that I had just returned. That had witnessed the shelling and that the B.B.C news reports were not accurate and could, in fact, cost lives. He listened as I told him about my friend Rada, who was currently in Osijek. She was half Serb and half Croat and had wanted to come to Baranja to stay with me. However, she was now hesitant because she had seen BBC News reports that Serbian fighters were killing all non–Serbs. That no one should try and go to Baranja unless they were 100% ethnically Serbian. I told him that this was, in fact, the Croatian not Serbian policy about Croatian ethnicity, residency, and jobs and that I had witnessed it. I further told him that Rada was in hiding with her daughter and said that she was too afraid to go anyway or stay so what should she do? The response from this excellent journalist and man was to tell me that he didn't have time to listen to my personal history and wasn't at all interested in discussing it further. I was furious, but felt utterly impotent and could only telephone Serbian friends in England to commiserate with them and offer my support in any way that may help.

CHAPTER TEN

I don't know how my mother tolerated my seemingly endless telephone conversations as they seemed to dominate my waking hours. Friends calling me, their friends enquiring about family members in Krajina, endless offers of aid if I could somehow arrange it. My darling Mum smiled through all of it, offering endless cups of coffee or tea and comforting words. She had absolutely no idea what her seemingly lunatic of a daughter had got herself into. Her telephone and television were in the same room and she gave up trying to watch it and took to reading a book. My behaviour on reflection was selfish and inconsiderate, but it didn't seem that way at the time and she never once raised any objections. I suddenly felt so drained and exhausted that I lost both my enthusiasm and energy to do anything. I felt I desperately needed some normality and then the idea of a holiday came to me.

Mum was probably absolutely delighted when I suddenly decided that Jude and I should take a holiday. Jude was still grieving over the death of Fred, her husband on December 13th of the previous year. She was semi-retired and found it hard to fill her days sometimes. I found an amazingly cheap offer for two for a Kenyan safari and beach holiday. We had to leave within the next two days and so I asked Jude to pop in for a quick chat on her way home from a shopping trip. Telling her, she should sit down because I had some important news! 'Do you fancy a holiday Jude?' 'Yes, that would be great' She replied. 'Ok then we leave the day after tomorrow, a weeks safari in Kenya followed by a week in Mombassa by the beach' said I grinning as her eyes suddenly widened. Now everyone who knows Jude well knows that she needs four days to pack, a day for the hairdresser, another day at the nail clinic and four more days to think about it. We made it to the airport and flew off on our great adventure. We thought it would end almost immediately when the pilot aborted his landing in Bahrein and a planeful of passengers screamed in terror as he suddenly rose steeply from the runway. Jude and I didn't scream, only foreigners do that we concurred, but were gripping each other's hand very tightly. We made it safely to Kenya and landed at Nairobi airport.

This wasn't my first safari and the way the lions were always conveniently laying around under the same tree every day made me wonder if they were actually on a leash. I suspected they were fed there, but I didn't spoil it for Jude who loved it. Loved it that is, apart from the bit where a large bull elephant charged our minibus. My love of cats and pity for the stray ones in evidence at the beach resort in Mombassa very nearly strained our friendship. I noticed a cat (one of Ilija's homeless persons) hanging around outside the restaurant on our first evening there and naturally saved a little meat in my paper napkin for it. Outside, on our way to the bar after dinner, the little cat gratefully took the meat from me and it was then I noticed that she was obviously nursing kittens. They duly appeared a few moments later. At breakfast the next morning as we helped ourselves to the buffet I was ahead of Judith and took an enormous portion of bacon and four sausages. Judith, following on behind, looked at me in amazement. 'Take bacon and sausage' I hissed at her. 'Oh no, I can't eat that so early in the morning, was her reply. 'No, it's for me' I answered. She gave me a somewhat worried look, duly took a pile of bacon and sausage, asked me if I wanted tomatoes too and then followed me back to our table. 'Are you quite mad?' She enquired. 'If you eat all that I shall think you caught worms somewhere.' I now explained that it wasn't for me but for the cat outside. She groaned audibly. 'Well, you needn't think that I am walking outside with a plate!' 'Of course not! Put it in your paper serviette but don't let anyone see you' Jude was not at all pleased with me. There we sat in this beautiful restaurant, in a luxurious hotel, with waiters hovering. They responded to the merest glance in their direction and it was quite difficult to secrete the bacon and sausage in our paper napkins. We succeeded, but as we left the restaurant, Jude rounded on me furiously and told me that she was absolutely not going to do that at every meal for the damn cat. That the damn cat had managed to survive before we arrived and no doubt the damn cat would survive after we left. But she did do it and we left a nicely rounded mother cat who, hopefully, was fed by others who followed us! We were staying in wonderful little thatched houses built around trees. There was a terrace where we often sat in the evenings and enjoyed our daily, complimentary basket of fruit. Judith could now take sweet revenge on me because I am a little afraid of monkeys. She did what all the notices warned against and fed them bits of fruit. As a result, they often came hurtling onto the veranda to beg for more. Now what Jude had forgotten was that if I get stressed, I have nightmares. Lone behold, one night I leapt out of bed, shook her awake and screamed that there was a monkey behind the wardrobe. An intrepid Jude ordered me into the bathroom and began to hunt about the room and then on the balcony. My mind cleared as I stood there looking at myself in the mirror and I went out to tell her that I thought I had actually dreamt it. We had some wonderful memories of our holiday, sailing out to a sand bar for the day and to a small island for lunch another day. That idyllic setting was somewhat spoiled when we followed another's gaze upwards. For hanging from the thatched roof of the little restaurant, was a colony of bats all sleeping in the noonday sun! Fascinating, but not really an ideal dining location and we kept patting the top of our heads just to check nothing was dropping on them.

I so enjoyed our time together, now feeling much refreshed and ready to face the World again. Jude is an amazing friend and joined in the challenge to collect aid for Baranja. She also handled an enormous amount of correspondence for me when I was contributing to the Serbian lobby in London. She even took it all in her stride when a sinister-looking man was seen hanging around outside her home after I had left for Serbia the following month. Her neighbours also noticed him and were going to alert the police. However, he disappeared and wasn't seen again. I was to receive a visit from a member of Britain's intelligence service the following year. He asked me what I was doing, about conditions in Serbia and similar questions. I didn't hold back! I gave him a complete history dating back to 1987, followed by a history of Serbia as an ally of the British during the First World War, then the Second World War. Then he got a lecture on Croatia's role in those Wars, their fascist past, and fascist future if Tudjman had anything to do with it. My darling, Mum kept the tea flowing and this rather nice if somewhat bemused representative of Her Majesty's security service left never to return!

I had a telephone call from someone called John Kennedy from Ian Greer Associates. He told me that he had read with interest my letter to the Times commenting on the standard of the news items regarding Baranja. He asked me if I would be willing to go up to see him in London. I was eager to help in any way I could and agreed to meet him. Had I known then what I know now, I would have claimed expenses for this and the coming trips. He was a lobbyist and was no doubt paid vast sums of money while people like me who were contributing our time and energy were spending money that we could ill-afford on travel and telephone expenses. In the event, I met him at his offices in central London, I can't recall now where they were. I subsequently had another meeting with a group of perhaps twelve or so others who were members of the Serbian Lobby. I gave permission for them to circulate amongst the members of Parliament a statement I had made recording the events of 1990 I had witnessed when I had been in Osijek. I was then asked to join speakers in one of the anti-rooms in the House of Commons in the British Parliament to read this statement. There seemed to be several hundred in the audience which was made up of members of Parliament, other interested parties and probably the press.

I shared the platform with some people whom as I got to know them found to be extremely dedicated and very well-respected people in their field. One of these was the late Michael Lees, a British secret agent who had fought with General Mihailovic in the Second World

War. He was a delightful man who had dedicated his life to trying to right the injustices and betrayal, as he saw them, visited upon the Chetniks and their leader Mihalilovic. The late H.R.H.Prince Tomislav Karadjordjevic was also there. I had enormous respect for the prince. He was a gentleman and unfailingly courteous and worked hard for his country of birth which it was clear he loved. He was the only male member of his royal line that I admired. Some others I met were extremely unimpressive and downright arrogant and one bore a striking resemblance to an English bank manager.

I had no idea that a publicist company involved with this Serbian lobby would be embroiled in a 'cash for questions' scandal which involved a British member of Parliament being paid to ask questions in the House of Commons. This part of the proceedings in Parliament is part of the Members job, for which he is paid a salary. Being called by the speaker and standing up before all the Members of the House to ask a question publicizes that particular subject. Being paid to ask questions is highly improper. This link in my view debased a very worthy cause and most of my fellow members and I were totally unaware of it. No one ever paid me for my work with the lobby and the travel and telephone expenses I incurred on their behalf were not inconsiderable.

Both before and after the holiday Jude accompanied me to meet Serbian communities in Derby and London to discuss fund-raising and also news about Baranja. Jude is an excellent judge of character, far more than I and her support and suggestions were just what I needed. She had been a guest in Baranja, had met many people there, but was in many respects neutral and gave me some valuable, well-balanced opinions. Some of the people we met gave me the addresses of their relatives or friends in Krajina and asked me to contact them or pass on letters.

One of the dearest men I met was Srbobran Krnjulac, who lived in Coventry. Later, he and I began to work more closely together especially in gathering aid for Baranja.

I was now approached by one of John Kennedy's representatives, a woman called Anne, who asked me if I would send regular reports back to them when I returned to Baranja. They wanted me to gather anything that would help the Serbian people to show the World just how much they were suffering and how they were wrongly accused and much maligned as a nation. I was handed some important telephone numbers in Serbia of influential people that would help me if I needed it. One of them was the for the secretary to President Milosevic. Others were army generals in Belgrade.

I was not then, nor have I ever, been interested in politics other than my personal point of view. I am, I suppose, a middle of the road Socialist. I firmly believe in the government of the people, by the people, for the people. Which means that the nation's government, army and police force must all be fully accountable to their people and work for them not control them. My late father was a trade union official and my late brother was a lawyer who worked for the legal rights of workers and also of the disabled. He was instrumental in the preparation and implementation of the compensation law regarding Pneumoconiosis, a chronic lung disease that affects many miners. I was taught to stand up for what I thought was right. To fight the curse of bigotry and racism as my brother and father had and I am immensely proud of the way they tried to do this.

However, my dearest brother Simon was also quintessentially British and not prone to over dramatisation or overt displays of patriotism. He would be amused, I am sure, to read such praise from a little sister who, with her teasing, used to infuriate him. Nevertheless, he was always on hand to help me at times of real crisis. And it was in London in December 1991 that I called him to ask him for his help. Ilija had often complained about the fact that they had no night scopes and were severely disadvantaged by this when they were on patrol in the forests around Kopachski. The night scope would give them infrared images of any warm-blooded creatures or persons hidden in the darkness. I met Simon at his offices in central London. We strolled into Regent's Street as I explained to him what I needed his advice on. I thought that he probably knew more about binoculars and telescopes than me and I was right. He led me to an enormous shop specializing in all sorts of optical instruments and as we were looking in the window of the shop, he asked me what I wanted to buy. 'A night scope for Ilija' I said. 'Yes dear,' came his kindly response. 'But, what does he want to use it for?' 'Well', I began, 'when he is on patrol in the forest at night, he must be able to see if there are any soldiers waiting to ambush them. This would allow him to shoot first.'

My dear, kind brother blanched. 'Oh good god! Please do not say that in this shop! Give another reason, bird-watching, he likes bird-watching!' I wanted to giggle, but I dared not. We stepped inside the shop and the assistant came forward to help us. 'I would like a night scope please' I explained, 'not too big, powerful but able to be fit in a small rucksack.' Simon was moving away from me to examine something he suddenly found fascinating further into the shop. Now came the question 'What do you want to use it for?' 'Bird-watching, my husbands likes bird-watching' I replied confidently. 'At night madam? He watches birds at night?' He enquired. A bit superior I thought for a salesman. 'Owls' I said, 'Owls, he likes to watch them.' Before he could start quizzing me on impossible questions such as how far away the owl would be, or how high up in the tree I quickly called Simon over. I left the purchase to him, handing over my credit card and number. Simon then amazed me as he often did. He was carrying a handheld day scope which had a carrying strap. Directing the assistant to add it to the invoice, he handed me back my card. 'My pleasure' he said 'a little contribution to your cause, God help you.' These scopes found their way to Ilija within a week of their purchase with the aid of a friendly Jat pilot and lots of friends of friends!

On December the 20th, 1991 I again travelled up to London, this time, accompanying my parents to attend Simon's 50th birthday celebrations. He and his family had a lovely big house in North London and were expecting lots of guests. Simon drew me aside and asked me not to ambush some of his politician friends on behalf of the Serbian lobby. They were members of the Labour Opposition party at this time. Margaret Thatcher's Tories held power. I knew that she was not a friend of Serbia. I had written to her at Downing Street and while she at least dictated a reply, the page positively spat venom. She was unaware that Croatia had a fascist regime and while Croatia may have been guilty of some war crimes during the 2nd World War, so was Serbia. I couldn't believe my eyes, here was a graduate of Oxford who was utterly ignorant of European history! During the miner strikes of 1984, the British police engaged in an orgy of violence against men trying to protect their jobs. Deaths, mass arrests, jailings, and sackings, were employed in her quest to smash the might of the unions. She led her government in the use of the most shameful anti-democratic measures. There were roadblocks, manipulation of the state media and even the justice system in her determination to win what she saw as a class war. She had intended to bring charges of seditious insurrection against the left-wing councils of Liverpool and London and even decided to level these charges at the whole of the Opposition Labour Party. Only the Brighton bombing of her hotel at the Tory Party Annual Conference stopped her. She was a figure of intense hatred to the working man. And a great admirer of Franjo Tudjman. There was no point whatsoever in appealing to her. But at the time, I was not aware of that and we just kept on trying!

I sidled up to many of Simon's party guests to see if I could direct the conversation towards the plight of the Serbs in Croatia. One or two of the guest responded, but I felt that after Simon's kindness with the scope it would have been churlish and boorish to ignore his earlier pleas. It had been very hard to pass up such an opportunity because there had been a change in me. I was no longer involved in the lobby merely for Ilija's sake. Now I was utterly committed to the job of making my own countryman understand the terrible injustices being enacted against the people of Yugoslavia particularly, but not exclusively, the Serbian people. Germany wanted reunification and the World stood back and applauded. Could the European major powers be fearful that a powerful Yugoslavia would in some way change the balance of power? They could not have been ignorant of the turmoil and tragedy such a break-up would bring to so many innocents. Who were arming Croatia? Yugoslavia had, had a highly lucrative armaments industry and exported to many parts of the

World. I suppose some of my anger was frustration because what impact could one tiny voice have amidst all the bellowing?

I was now in regular contact with Ilija and his calls no matter how brief gave me some kind of reassurance that he was safe and well. I was again spending many hours writing articles and lobbying members of parliament. When I was invited to SkyNews, to be interviewed by the respected presenter Bob Friend on their 6 p.m. news programme, I rushed out to buy something to wear. I must now admit that I was never phased about being interviewed on radio and television programmes, or even when I did my first public speaking in the precincts of the House of Commons. No, the what to wear question is the one that is certain to send me into a spin! Sky News sent a chauffeur-driven car to collect me from home and deliver me to the studios. Then I was shown to a make-up room where I had more eye makeup and lip gloss applied. Finally, a young woman came and led me into the studio. It was quite strange to see only the interviewer and me in the room, the cameras didn't have an operator but seemed to be fixed and remotely controlled. Bob Friend was a most charming man. His short introduction gave the viewer the information about my having recently returned from war-torn Yugoslavia. That the area I had been to have little food or electricity and how difficult life must be there. He opened the interview with me by asking me about what sort of food I had cooked there under such testing conditions. I didn't have the least intention of discussing cooking and so I gave a brief answer. Trying again, he now asked me about how relieved I must feel to be home safe and sound again. I now jumped in with both feet and told him that the emotion I felt was anger, not relief because of the mendacity of some news reports. At last, he asked me 'Well would you like to tell us about what happened to you?' I had learned my statement to members of Parliament almost word for word. It was based on the letters I had written about my experiences in Osijek with the paramilitaries and the need for us to leave in the middle of the night, fearing for our safety. And now I was able to use it again to tell my story to Bob Friend. I don't think he expected that at all and looked faintly bemused.

And then suddenly it was over and while the commercials ran I was whisked off down a few corridors, out through a door and there was a car waiting to take me home. It was rather frustrating because no one I knew actually had a sky box and so there was no one to ask about their impressions of the interview. I arrived home in time for some supper and told Mum all about it. She said 'That's nice dear, now be a sweetheart and make us some tea, there is an excellent series on that we can watch.' I didn't dare pick up the telephone, for Mum had just told me as plainly as she ever would that she would like to watch her TV show! I wasn't to know it, but this was to be the quiet before the storm and in the next few days my life was turned upside down.

CHAPTER ELEVEN

Around the 12th January 1992, I was on a flight back to Belgrade in Yugoslavia. I had received a telegram from Ilija's commanding officer that he was in prison in Sombor in Serbia. I was to be met by members of 'Matica Krajina' or 'Krajina Society.' It was an ex-pat organisation for Serbians from Krajina providing cultural, religious and other links.They took me directly to their office in Belgrade and all the staff there were incredibly kind and offered to assist me in any way they could. Most of them could speak a little English, but an older woman was the one who now took charge of the situation. She organized some coffee for me and we sat together to discuss the situation. I confessed that I had no idea what was happening or why Ilija would have been arrested. That he was a good man, had fought bravely in the recent fighting and had only just recovered after being wounded in action. Now she dropped their bombshell. Your husband has been arrested with the other 18 members of his unit and been charged with the murder of a Serb. They have all been sentenced to 16 year's imprisonment. I began to shake and was in total shock. All I could say was that it wasn't possible that Ilija would murder anyone and that I just didn't believe it. The woman told me that they knew of my work for the Serbian lobby and were so sorry about the present predicament I found myself in. They had organized a taxi to take me to Sombor where they suggested that I might be able to resolve any questions I had by visiting the prison holding Ilija.

I left Belgrade in the taxi around eight in the evening and the driver took the motorway North. I didn't feel like talking and fell asleep for most of the journey. We arrived in Sombor around ten-thirty that evening and I asked the driver to find me a hotel. We drove around the town for about half-an-hour trying in vain to find a hotel that was open and had vacancies. The driver was getting very nervous and I was able to understand that he had been called up by the Yugoslavian Army and had to report the next morning at 6 a.m. He asked if I minded transferring to a local taxi so that he could return to Belgrade and I gladly agreed. Poor man, he was so worried! I was still cheerful and supposed that a local taxi driver would know where the hotels were and I would soon find myself one. We drove for an hour, in another fruitless search for a hotel, he even drove me to Apatin a town about 19 km away. By now it was well after midnight and then we saw a motel with a light in the reception area. My driver got out and was met outside the door of the office by a large, scruffy individual who was obviously drunk. I got out of the car now and the scruffy man was telling the taxi driver to give me to him he would look after me. Tired, cold and frightened out of my wits, I felt the sobs building up and cried out to the driver to please, please not leave me there. The driver got back behind the wheel and told me that 'of course' he wouldn't leave me in a place like that. Now I asked him to take me to the nearest police station. I thought it would be far safer to sit in a police station all night than to stay in some dodgy hotel. The first thought that always came uppermost in my mind in grim situations was always 'I am so glad my Mother can't see what I am doing'.

The taxi driver suggested we go for coffee so that he could find a telephone because he had an idea. The coffee tasted wonderful and revived and warmed me. As I enjoyed it, I pretended not to be listening to the conversation my taxi-driver, who I now knew as Boro, was having with someone I assumed was probably his wife. Although he had his back turned to me, I could hear her yelling at him but couldn't make out yet whether I had safe digs for the night or not. Eventually, he turned round, smiled and told me that his wife would be happy to welcome me to their home. 'Ouch,' I thought what is this going to be like. His wife turned out to be a middle-aged, slightly stout lady who welcomed me with a huge hug and a table laid with fresh bread, smoked sausage, ham, fresh cheese, and gherkins. I thanked her profusely and tried to explain in the most uncomplicated way I could that my husband was in prison. I felt that I could hardly describe him as my boyfriend, fella or lover and I have always thought the term partner as ridiculous. I wonder why there isn't a really suitable word to describe the man you are living with unwed? The eternal fiancee doesn't somehow quite fit the bill. Perhaps someone will introduce wifette and husbandette into the language one day, after all, we have ladette? I was free to marry at this time, but things were complicated enough without planning a wedding. This dear lady now showed me to my bed for the night. It was an enormous bed, with great, stuffed pillows and a voluminous feather duvet. All the covers were stiffly starched, white cotton and I hardly dared get into bed for fear of creasing them! As soon as I snuggled down under the duvet, I fell fast asleep and slept soundly until I was roused for breakfast.

Bright and early I was knocking on the door of Sombor Prison. They flatly refused to let me see Ilija because I didn't have an official permit from the judge who had signed his arrest warrant. I made such a fuss that they, at least, let Ilija talk to me from behind the door. He told me that they had all been arrested and that Kostich, who had been reinstated as chief of police in Darda, was behind their detention. He asked me to return to Beli Manastir and obtain a permit to visit him from the judge there. Then he asked me if I would kindly buy some fruit and cigarettes for them which I did. I longed to be able to hug him and to see how he looked. But, they flatly refused to allow me in and so I promised to return the next day if I possibly could. Having given my grateful thanks to Boro's kindly wife I said my goodbyes and set off with her husband for Baranja.

I passed through the Serbian police controls at the bridge in Batina without a problem. But, when I got to the Krajina or Baranja side the police ordered Boro to drive me directly to the police headquarters in Beli Manastir and not let me out anywhere else. The only person I recognized at the police headquarters was a friend of Ilija's whose nickname was Fritz. No one spoke English and my Serbian was very basic. However, the police chief of Beli Manastir showed me to his office and indicated the telephone. He was a professional policeman who had been sacked from his position by the Croats and then reinstalled by the Serbs after August 1991. The chief knew my name and that I lived with Ilija, he was extremely kind and offered me sandwiches and a hot drink. I telephoned John Kennedy in London to explain my difficulties and he assured me he would try to help in whatever way possible. The police chief indicated to Fritz that I had a current visa and was free to stay in Baranja, but I needed an address. Unbeknown to me the house where all my furniture and belongings were, where Ilija and I had been staying, had been rigged with booby-traps by friends of Ilija's to prevent looters from stealing our belongings. I later saw on the door a notice saying 'If you wish to meet God come in.' Fritz offered to let me move in with his family and I gratefully accepted his offer. The next day I went to see the head judge and obtained a permit to visit Ilija in jail and with great kindness, Fritz told me he would drive me to Sombor prison in Serbia.

I was greatly relieved to be shown into the visitor's room to see Ilija. There was a metal grille between us and so it was impossible to embrace. He was extremely pale and after we had greeted each other, as best we could, he asked me if I were willing or able to help him. He kept saying, we did nothing, they did all their tests and know that we are innocent but are saying we will serve 16 years here. He looked so devastated I immediately became very brisk and business-like and told him not to be so dramatic, of course, he wouldn't and I would get him out. Fortunately, I had the foresight to take a notepad and pen with me and now I asked him to tell me what had happened and whatever he knew about why he was here.

On the morning of 31st December 1991, Ilija was on duty with the police special forces unit who were first responders to any attack by the Croatian military. The Beli Manastir police chief called Ilija into his office. He told him to take some of his men and go and arrest the three men that he believed were involved in the murder of Croatians in Cheminac. The regular police force criminal investigators of Beli Manastir were unwilling to go into the villages and confront anyone about the murders of Croatian civilians. Although such arrests of suspects were not part of Ilija's units responsibilities, they agreed to do it.

During that month, fifteen men had disappeared and later their bodies had been found, in the village of Cheminac. Information from police sources had implicated three men who were ethnic Serb refugees from Bilogora in Croatia. They had been part of a large group of refugees, men, women and children, who had arrived from Croatia, via Bosnia, having been expelled from their villages by Croatian paramilitaries. 27 Serbian villages had been burnt to the ground and there had been many killings. These refugees had been housed by the Red Cross in Cheminac village which had been abandoned by its former residents except for perhaps some 40 Croatians who had stayed on their farms. The men from Bilogora were required to join the Territorials and were armed by the new Krajina army. There were three separate armed groups in Baranja at this time; The Yugoslavian Army, who was confined to barracks by order of their generals. The local Territorial Defence Force formed from civilian conscripts, refugees, and senior citizens. And the Police force made up of 3 departments; traffic, criminal and special forces. The special forces fought on the front lines in the event of a Croatian attack. Ilija was a member of these special forces.

The Bilogora refugees were believed to have arrived in the middle of the previous November and the killings in Cheminac began at the beginning of December. The father of one of Ilija's friend was a victim of these murderers and had been found in the bottom of his own well. His son, Darko S. had been the keyboard player with Ilija playing guitar in a band they started together in the late 70's. Tragically, Darko had died in 1978 aged 22 years old. Ilija knew the family very well and was both saddened and furiously angry. Not just at the murder of his friend's father, but at the other brutal slayings of entirely innocent Croats who had wanted to stay and look after their farms. Even worse in Ilija's mind was that he had urged many of them in mid and late September to stay. He had been confident that since none had been extremists and terrorized Serbian families, he could assure them that nothing would happen to them, not dreaming that these newcomers would wage war against all Croats. Whether their motive was revenge or robbery was unknown.

At around 10 a.m. on the morning of the 31st December 1991, Ilija and three others arrived outside the address in Cheminac, which the police chief had given them. One of the men immediately left the group saying that he had to see someone in the village. The remaining men including Ilija then arrested the first suspect from the address without any trouble. The second suspect lived opposite the first and he too was detained and brought to stand with the first suspect. At that moment, they were fired on from some of the houses nearby by other Bilogora refugees trying to prevent the arrests. In the confusion, one of the policemen, despite being ordered not to fire, panicked and returned fire. They put the prisoners into their jeep and quickly drove off back to Beli Manastir. They handed the prisoners over at police headquarters and as they were being taken down to the cells one of the men complained that he felt unwell. They discovered he had a bullet wound and was immediately taken to hospital in Sombor. Ilija and his men returned to duty, the fourth man returned from Cheminac about an hour later. Just before this fourth man returned Ilija was given the news by one of the policemen that the prisoner had died soon after his arrival in Sombor hospital. And that he had two bullet wounds, one from a shotgun and one from an assault rifle. Ilija was astounded because there had been no evidence of blood in the vehicle and although the man had not spoken, had been fully conscious and hadn't appeared to be injured in any way. Even the other prisoner sitting next to him had been unaware of his injuries.

At midday, there now came more serious news. A group of around fifty, armed Bilogora refugees from Cheminac were marching on Beli Manastir Police Headquarters to demand the arrest of all 19 members of one unit of the special forces. They claimed that they had been warned by the other police chief (Kostich in Darda) that this unit of the special police forces would attack and kill all the Bilogora refugees in Cheminac.

This just happened to be Ilija's unit who were investigating the killings of Croatians in Cheminac. It also happened to be the same unit who had tried to prevent Kostich from looting Beli Manastir and stealing the Petrol and oil reserves. Kostich wanted to destroy this particular unit because most of them were the original group of 19 who had been in the first fire-fight on 18ᵗʰ August. They, unlike others and even the policemen in Beli Manastir, were not afraid of Kostich and fully prepared to stand up to him.

The Beli Manastir police chief told Ilija that he would have to arrest him and the three others in his group while the death of a refugee was investigated. Ilija's response was to tell him that since they had done absolutely nothing wrong and had not shot the man, they would submit themselves to whatever investigation was necessary. Ilija and the others were taken to Novi Sad in Serbia the following day to check for gunpowder residue on their hands or clothing. Their guns were tested to see if they had been fired and then the bullets for comparison with those recovered from the body. Special Police forces did not carry shotguns and so they had nothing to check regards that from the police. Within days, the reports returned that three of the four guns had not been fired, but one had. There was no gunpowder residue on three of the four men tested. The fourth man had opened fire but at their attackers and it was Ilija's belief that in trying to free them, the other refugees had inadvertently shot their friend. Especially because they had shotguns in addition to their AK47's, unlike the Special Police Units.

However, now Kostich was doing all in his power to see that the unit would stay in jail in Serbia for now all 19 had been arrested. The remaining Bilogora murder suspect, who Ilija had detained on that fateful day, had been released without charge. No one attempted to go and seize any weapons or shotguns from the Bilogora refugees in Cheminac to be tested against the bullets that killed their friend. And very shortly around a further ten suspects in the mass killings and their families, left Cheminac and disappeared to live outside

Baranja, possibly emigrating. Afterwards, the murders ceased and the remaining refugees went about their daily lives trying to build a new life for themselves in Cheminac.

I took down everything Ilija had told me and noted the names of all the nineteen men arrested. They had not yet been tried and so the news I had been greeted with about a sixteen-year-sentence wasn't accurate. Nevertheless, I was anxious about how on earth I could help them all. None of Ilija's friends wanted to know anything about what was happening to him or the others. I was really disgusted, but Fritz,(Nebojsha's nickname because with his blond hair everyone thought he looked German), was a staunch ally on whom I could rely. I telephoned my contact in John Kennedy's office and relayed to them what I had been told by Ilija. I also told them that I could not now do my work collecting witness statements or photograph bomb damage. Nor could I take the survivors accounts of a massacre that had happened in a Roma town called Torijanci in December. Over the next few days, I again went to see a judge in Beli Manastir to put the case for their innocence along with the sister of another imprisoned man. I got several updates from John Kennedy's office and finally, on the 17th January, I got a message from them that Ilija would be released the next day. Fritz drove me to the prison to give Ilija the good news and he immediately said that he would not leave his men behind in jail. They would have to release them all because all of them were innocent of any crime. I relayed the news to John Kennedy's office and waited.

All 19 were eventually released on the 23rd January 1992. There were no charges to answer. The man that had panicked and opened fire was also not charged. Fortunately, the judge realized that if the Bilogora refugees had not opened fire on the police unit, no one would have been hurt. These actions, however, were terrible indictments against the police chief, policemen, and justices. They pursued the death of a Serbian refugee with the vigour and correctness one would associate with every efficient police service. Yet they chose to ignore the murders of no less than 15 Croatian men brutally murdered in Cheminac and others that were killed in other local villages, numbering around 120. The numbers were not known because they were not investigated especially not those in Bilje, which Kostich controlled. These people were not killed in the initial fighting but by criminals trying to steal and rob or refugees enacting revenge or psychopaths, they all surface when law and order break down. These acts could never be justified and brings shame on those that perpetrated them and those that refused to bring the guilty ones to justice. Yes, terrible things had happened to Bilogora refugees in Croatia and to Serbs in Osijek, Virovitica, and may other towns in Croatia. But that can never justify what some of them did in Cheminac, Beli Manastir, Karanac, Grabovac, kozarac, Bilje and other villages.

When Ilija returned home, he now told me more about Kostich the Darda police chief and warned me that this man may try again to destroy his unit. He had made two previous attempts before the recent arrests of Ilija and his unit. The first attempt was Ilija and the men were returning from the front line at Kopachski Rit, the village at the edge of the Kopachski National Park. Ilija said they were warned that Kostich was waiting to ambush the unit between Suza and Sokolovac villages. And so his unit took a different route back to Beli Manastir. Kostich's henchmen were several high ranking army officers, Lt. Colonels and above. This group had become immensely rich from the systematic pillaging of Baranja. Kostich and these men spread the rumour that it was the Police special forces who were the source of all the problems in the area.They thought they would be excellent scapegoats for their criminal enterprises.

The next attempt by Kostich, this time with the collusion of these army henchmen, very nearly succeeded in killing all 48 members of the Police special forces. The force was called on to respond to an attack by the Croatian army at Devil's Bridge, just inside Baranja near the town of Osijek in Croatia. At around mid-day on the 18th December 1991, a large number of Croatian soldiers advanced into the area of Baranja known as Devil's Bridge. There was dense fog and the special forces, having been ordered to take plenty of ammunition because they were facing a significant number of Croatian soldiers took up their defensive positions. They had been ordered to take the centre position. Around 100, Yugoslavian Army soldiers from Shabac took up a position to their right and on the left there were around 80 territorial reservists and around 15 men of the Darda police force. By 4 p.m., it was dark and the two sides exchanged sporadic fire. Mortars and rocket- propelled grenades were used by both sides.

At around 2 a.m in the morning of the 19ᵗʰ December, Scouts of Ilija's group went to check on the situation on the left and right flanks. They discovered that both the Yugoslavian Army soldiers defending the right flank and the Territorials and Darda police on the left flank had all withdrawn. The 48 of them realised that they were alone and so their commander Milan J. tried to contact the army command who instructed him to stay and defend the position at all costs. These 48 now regrouped to cover the areas as best they could. At first light around 8 a.m., the Croatians launched a full-scale attack. As the fighting continued, after around 3 hours the Special Police found they were running out of ammunition and sent 3 runners to try and get more and also to get help. The got the ammunition and got a message to the men in Beli Manastir that they were in dire straits and needed help. Beli Manastir sent 140 armed police and police reservists by bus to Devil's Bridge but via Darda where Kostich and the Army officers stopped them and told them their help wasn't necessary. That the men had been resupplied and that everything was under control. Meanwhile, the three men returned with the ammunition but the group was under such concentrated fire and attack they began to retreat. The decision was made that they had to break out because they were now encircled. The order was given and as a man, the 48 of them charged through the Croatian lines and made it to their vehicles. One of their number, Milan Stular, was shot and died instantly, but they managed to carry him with them. They made it back to their vehicles and drove back to Knezevi Vinogradi. There they confronted the Army officers who had withdrawn all their soldiers. The colonel in charge finally apologized to them and tried to explain that he had been given the wrong information. But it has to be said, the anger of some of these men at their betrayal resulted in all the army officers being severely beaten and they were lucky they were not shot. Instead, the Special Police Units left and returned to a hero's welcome in Beli Manastir. The Croatians had suffered heavy losses and the army recaptured the position later in the day.

After the release of Ilija and the fellow men of his unit, the Special Police Units were disbanded and were now made members of the army pioneer force guarding the front lines. Kostich had his way. But at least, he never gained control of the Beli Manastir police force.

CHAPTER TWELVE

There are so many negatives about this time of mine in Beli Manastir in 1992. I now learned the fate of my dear shogur and friend Franjo.

As a committed supporter of a united Yugoslavia and a socialist, Franjo would have no truck with the new right-wing political parties that were emerging during the late 1980's. Although an atheist, he was tolerant of others religious beliefs and celebrations and his Serbian wife always celebrated Orthodox holy days. He even made a donation to the restoration fund of the local Roman Catholic Church, because he saw this as part of his village's heritage and something to be preserved. He had been a good footballer in his youth and later a referee for the local teams. He was a professor of political science and worked for a local company, Belje. He farmed his share of his family's 15 acres of farmland. Always a generous man he even sponsored a young relative at medical school in Zagreb. I didn't know about any of this at that time. I just loved him for his endless acts of kindness towards us and remember a pair of twinkling blue eyes and a smiling face. He was someone who loved to talk about his farm and tell us funny stories about his village and its people. His favourite subject was History. Politics were never on the agenda. He was so very proud of Yugoslavia and all its achievements It was to his eternal regret that he had no children because his only child had died when he was 7 years old. The tensions caused by this tragedy and civil war resulted in him and his wife Maria separating in 1991. He was for many years a member of the local Municipal Council, highly respected and known for his honesty and integrity. After the elections, bringing the HDZ to power in Croatia in 1990 the paramilitary wing of the party called ZNG, known as Zengi and HOSS began to harass non-Serbs living in Baranja and Croatia. Serbians were their main target and they strutted through the towns and villages in their black uniforms, emulating their heroes, Hitler's brown-shirted storm troopers. Some residents became so afraid of the mostly night- time terror that they spent their nights at Franjo's farm, under his protection and so he incurred the wrath of the Zengi and HOSS.

When the civil war began in Baranja in August of 1991, Franjo did not leave with the retreating Zengi forces and many Croatian civilians who fled to Osijek. He believed that Croatian Nationalism was nothing to do with him and that eventually, people would come to their senses and be able to co-exist together or that Baranja would become independent of both Croatia and Serbia. In either event, he felt he could stay in his own home which he had largely built himself. Now the ugly and vicious face of extremism was exposed because a group of recently arrived Bilogori Serbian refugees and shockingly, one of his neighbours, began a vendetta against him. Like so many others that we knew, the neighbour, of mixed ethnicity, thought, because of his own insane instability, that he had to prove his unswerving loyalty to whichever side he chose. Many on both sides became the most rabid extremists, guilty of some of the worst excesses.

Despite attempts by loyal friends and by Ilija, who tried desperately to protect him, these cowards made their deadly attacks at night. They threw grenades into his garden and made threats to kill him if he didn't leave, simply because he was Croatian. By December 1991, Franjo had decided to leave and go to Croatia. His aged mother, who was living near Zagreb, wanted to see him and sadly he now found life in Baranja intolerable. Devastated that some of his closest friends had turned on him, he crossed the Hungarian border in mid-December of 1991 and made his way to Zagreb. His wife Maria had moved back in with her family in Beli Manastir and nowadays I rarely saw her. On my return in 1992, I asked Ilija if he knew where and how Franjo was, but Ilija had no way of finding anything out about him now that he was in Croatia.

Beli Manastir now in January of 1992 looked quite desolate. It was an extremely, cold winter with icy fog during the day and freezing nights. Fortunately, most houses had wood burning stoves and we were able to cook on these because the men made sure each house had firewood. I had returned to the house in Beli Manastir, where my furniture and belonging were after the booby traps had been disarmed. Ilija now was part of an army unit of the R.S.K, Republika Srpska Krajina (Serbian Army of Krajina). And when not on frontline duties he patrolled the streets of Beli Manastir. We were now contacted by some families who were subjected to threats and violence because they were Croatian. Most, but not all of these threats came from refugees or petty criminals who were trying to force families to leave their homes or businesses. These people often wore military uniforms because they had been conscripted into the territorial or local defence units of the R.S.K. They had absolutely no authority over the civilian population and their role was to assist in the defence of the borders of Krajina. Their justification for trying to evict Croatians from their homes was always the same. They had been driven out of Croatia and their homes were burnt so why not do the same to these Croatians?

The problems for one family of Croatians, the Ratkajech family, who lived near the centre of the town started in late November of 1991.They had a large modern family house and a smaller, newer house had been built in their garden. They were a family of six, grandparents, parents and two young sons. They first came to Ilija's attention in early December 1991 when he was on patrol in the town. He and Fritz were passing the family's home when they saw the family standing in their garden, evidently in great distress, with two armed men in R.S.K uniform talking to them. Ilija, leaving Fritz in their jeep, went to investigate. The family were all weeping and Ilija went to the grandmother and asked her what was wrong. She told him that these two soldiers were ordering them to leave their home immediately. That they had nowhere to go and didn't know what to do. Ilija turned to the soldiers, two officers and asked them who they were. They gave their ranks as Captains and also their names. Ordering them to remain where they were Ilija quietly ushered the family back inside the larger of the two homes. 'What would you like to do?', he asked 'do you wish to stay or would you like to leave?'. 'Can we stay? asked the grandfather. 'I worked my whole life, here and in Germany to make these homes, I don't want to leave. But we are too afraid to stay here.' Ilija told them that of course they should stay if they wished and he would do everything he could to protect them.

Ilija now turned his attention to the two Army officers waiting outside. He described to me the cold fury he felt at seeing the distress of the family being held at gunpoint by two men in uniform. These two men had assumed that the family was defenceless, which they were and so they could, therefore, turn them out of their home on a freezing December day. All so that they could loot or move into, their beautiful home. Ilija promptly disarmed and arrested them and took them to the police headquarters. Here, Ilija wrote a report and gave it to his superiors. But Ilija knew that they would both be released and so he told them, plainly, to stay away from the family or face the consequences. He then returned to calm the Ratkajech family and when he was able, up until his arrest at the end of December, he visited them assisting them in any way that he could.

The situation at this time in Beli Manastir was that businesses that had been abandoned by their Croatian owners in August and September of 1991 were taken over and run by Serbs. This enabled the properties to remain intact and they began to provide a service to the community. The supermarket once again had a few food items for sale and most local cafes were operating again. This helped in some measure to provide employment. The theft and subsequent sale of the plant and machinery from many local factories left the employees without work and so unemployment was a major problem. The army and police forces in Krajina were paid at subsistence level only. However, there was no charge being levied at this time for telephone, water or electricity supplies, as infrequent as they were. The flour and milk company were working and most families relied on their relatives in the villages to supply much of their dairy and meat products. But times were hard and many were hungry. The Red Cross was supplying the refugee families with rations but not the local inhabitants. Bartering became a useful tool and in our street of 8 houses if anyone managed to buy some washing powder they would share it out amongst the other women.

One day, Ilija was given a large sack of cvarak, or scratchings; the crispy pieces of pork skin that are left after making lard. They were unfit for human consumption because they were too old. I was to ask my neighbour Dushanka if she would like them for her pigs. There is another word in the Serbian language, zvaka meaning chewing gum and for some reason, I used to confuse them. So I actually told Dushanka that I had a big bag of old chewing gum and would she like it for her pigs to eat. She looked at me in amazement saying, 'Maya!' (everyone calls me Maya here). 'Zvaka never gets too old to eat and I would never, ever feed it to my pigs! I will eat it thank you!' I gave Ilija the news and wondered at the idea of eating smelly, old Chvarak, but, who was I to judge, so Ilija delivered the sack and left it outside Dushanka's door. A little later Dushanka saw him in the street and asked why he had left bags of smelly old pork scratchings outside her door. 'Maja said you wanted it,' he replied. 'No, she asked me if I would like some old chewing gum!' came the reply. She fed it to her pigs!

We had a message from the Ratkajec family and again they seemed in deep distress. Ilija had been away for 3 weeks in Sombor and obviously had not been able to visit them. He took me to meet them and on the way I managed to buy some essentials for them including washing powder, soap, toothpaste and some basic food items. When we arrived, the family were gathered around a table. Until that day, I have never before witnessed an elderly man, perhaps in his seventies, totally unable to control his facial muscles. Only their son was calm the women were sobbing and the two small boys around 8 and 10 were confused and obviously very frightened. Grandfather told us of the abusive telephone call, threats and their fear of leaving the house, such fear that they had little or no food left.

145

Ilija explained why he hadn't been able to call earlier but now they had both of us to help them. I felt so ashamed to be part of something that reduced these decent, hardworking people to such terror. When I spoke to others, they again replied that this is what Serbs were suffering in Croatia. Ilija and I went straight to the Mayors office and spoke to Zivanovich. I begged him to go on the local radio and ask the community to stop these attacks on their neighbours. If they are retaliating against Croatian attacks on Serbs, don't they want to be better than that? Why don't they show the World that they can live alongside Croatians as they do Roma and Hungarians? Why should they let the criminals take over their society? Zivanovich shrugged and said that he couldn't do that. I felt a terrible sense of hopelessness and on the other hand fury. I took regular supplies of food, etc. to the Ratkajec family when it was possible and to other families in the same position as they. Some of the criminals spread the rumour that Ilija and I were charging families protection money, I suppose helping someone in the name of humanity was alien to them and, therefore, they should be pitied. One of the families in our street was Croatian. In November 1991, a group of four men dressed in police uniforms had tried to take their car. Ilija saw what was happening from our garden, grabbed his gun and confronted them. He told them to leave immediately and not to come back. The policemen were aware that all the Special Police forces were housed in this area of the town and quickly left never to be seen again.

There were still shells falling into Beli Manastir. Sometimes in the morning, which made shopping dangerous. I was only caught outside once when I was on my way to a local shop. I heard the familiar sound of the alarm forewarning of shelling. I was only a few streets away from home when my knee suddenly gave way. Putting down my bags, I looked around hoping to get some help and to my relief a friend was passing on his bicycle. He yelled at me to hurry home and asked me if I was alright. I yelled back that I wasn't and I needed help. He smiled gaily and rode off. He had gone to fetch Ilija. Fortunately, Ilija hadn't left for his tour of duty and rescued me and the shopping! The intermittent knee problem, a relic of years of playing sport, was a nuisance. I had about a 20-minute walk to the town centre and piazza to buy things when and as they were available and yet at this time I feared being caught outside during the shelling. Petrol rationing meant that we carefully conserved what little fuel we could buy and so I was unable to use our car for ordinary shopping trips.

We had frequent visits from the people looking for help, some Serbians some Croatians. I had brought some basic medicines from England that friends had collected, largely out of date but only by a couple of months. Sometimes I could only give them aspirin, but whatever they took, they were grateful for. There was also the regular sight of a horse and cart collecting anything that could be spared for the refugee families. We usually gave a set of one knife, fork, spoon, plate and cup. Until most of us were reduced to barely enough dishes and cutlery for ourselves. Once, in late Spring of 1992 my Croatian neighbour friend told me that she had been told that the Croatian Army would soon retake Baranja. And in that event, we should hide amongst the old blackened stems of the previous years sweetcorn. I think we all realized that leaving quickly was a distinct possibility.

When a group of young refugee conscripts came into Baranja and were housed in the school sports centre, we heard that they did not have any winter clothing. They had no boots only Wellingtons and so we women set about knitting socks, hats, and gloves for them. I even went to the Red Cross office to ask them if I could have some of the knitting wool I had seen in their stores. Jaeger knitting wool too! It contained alpaca and I thought it would make excellent socks for the young conscripts but my request was refused. Only civilians could receive Red Cross aid, not soldiers, but, if I had time would I consider knitting some jumpers for a family newly arrived from Croatia and in desperate need? I offered my services immediately, only to be told that there were eight children in the family with ages ranging from a toddler of two, up to a fifteen-year-old. There were just two colours of wool available black or white!! I knitted all eight jumpers trying hard to make each one individual! Ilija and I delivered them to the family and after we had knocked on their door, a face appeared, hands took the parcels and the door was firmly shut once more!! I admit I was irritated but who knows what these people had endured? We again turned our attention to the knitting and donating of socks.

At the end of January in 1992, we were asked to visit the scene of a massacre at Torjanci in the North East of Baranja on the border with Hungary. It had taken place several weeks previously in December of 1991. We were taken with an armed escort by the local Yugoslavian army on the orders of General Krstich, who was eager that I send out reports to the Serbian lobbyists in London.

Torjanci is a medium-sized village with the largest concentration of Roma in Baranja living there. Their neighbours were exclusively Croatian. Both the Roma and the Croatians were Roman Catholics, which is unusual regarding the Roma for most Balkan Roma are of the Orthodox religion. The border with Hungary in the Northern, Roma part of the village is less than 100 metres away from their houses. On our arrival, we were met by one of the Roma elders and as Ilija filmed us, he began to tell me their story of the killings and what had led up to them.

On the night before the attack Croatian soldiers, many former residents who had fled in August to Croatia infiltrated the village from Hungary. They were hidden in the houses of the Croatians who had stayed behind. Early the next morning, a baker from Beli Manastir came to deliver bread to the village and was shot dead on the road leading into it. The Croatian troops now went house to house in search of the Roma families. Some heard the screaming and shooting and fled towards the nearest Territorial Army reservists barracks to seek help. The reservists responded by forming a defensive line outside the village but did not enter. Meanwhile, in the village, some of the Roma men quickly took whatever weapons they had and locked themselves in their homes, but there was no time for any organized defence. The Croats rounded up about fifty or sixty men women and children and locked them in the school basement. One of the women shouted out to one of their captors, 'is it really you? You shared out table, you are our son's friend what are you doing?' The answer, they received from these Croatian soldiers, was this chilling message. 'Once we finish off the others we will come back to finish you off too.'

The Croats now went from house to house searching for anyone hiding and as they moved along the street one family who saw them coming tried escape. Their son aged 7 or 8 years old ran out into the road and was shot. His father ran to him and he was shot, then as his wife ran to kneel by both of them they shot her too. The sole survivor of this family had spent the night in Beli Manastir and so survived. This family was called Klash. As others tried to escape they were shot, men and women lying in their gardens or in the street. As the Croats hunted for more victims, Ilija and a group of 30 other Police Special Forces were already on their way alerted by the Territorials. As the Specials approached the village, they saw the Territorials who were lying in a drainage ditch. They told them they were not going to enter the village, but would stop the Croatians coming any further into Baranja. By now they were exchanging fire with some of these Croats. Ilija and the Specials decided that they had to take the risk to enter the village to try and rescue the Roma and to also prevent any more Croatians crossing from Hungary into Baranja. Piling into their jeeps, they drove at breakneck speed into the centre of the village.

Purely by chance, they stopped right outside the school and immediately opened fire on the Croats, who, unknown to them had the Roma families captive in the basement. They heard screams coming from this basement and opened it to check inside and the people immediately screamed louder in terror thinking they were about to be killed. The Specials calmed them, left two of the men to protect them and told them to stay there until it was safe to come out. Then they fanned out through the village and began to hunt down the Croatian soldiers, passing the bodies of the villagers as they did. Once the Territorials realized that the main fight was over they too now began to advance into the village. About an hour after the beginning of the fighting the Croats withdrew across the Hungarian border. There were Hungarian tanks, lorries, armoured vehicles and combat troops on the Hungarian side facing the Specials across no man's land. Their uniforms and insignia were clearly visible and their stance was menacing. It would be difficult to believe that they had not witnessed the murders of some of the Roma. No man's land between Hungary and Baranja had been mined. However, the day before the attack a local Croat had driven his flock of sheep across it, clearing a path to Hungary. The villagers had thought it was accidental at the time.

In all, some twenty or so Roma villagers and the baker had been murdered. The intent had been to kill all the non-ethnic Croatian villagers. The reason for this murderous assault on unarmed, innocent people was thought to have been part of the initial planning for the full-scale attack on Baranja mounted four months later in April 1992. It seemed a demonstration to all that no mercy would be shown to the residents of Baranja if Croatia had to take the area by force. There was a real fear amongst the population following the murders and they and the leaders of Baranja were desperate for everything to be made public.

I was now taken on a tour of the village to see the homes and places where the Roma had been killed. They took me to the house where Ilija had found a small boy, shaking in terror, hiding in a gap between a refrigerator and a wall. He had been discovered as they searched the village for victims or Croat paramilitaries. I then met some of the Roma women, one of them in her sixties, showed me her legs, and I could still see the scars and wounds she suffered as she crawled through the undergrowth to escape. Others showed me similar scars and all began to cry that many of their attackers were men they had known from childhood, had seen every day and gone to church with. They had wrongly assumed that because they were, like the majority of ethnic Croatians, Roman Catholic, that they would be safe. Why did they do this, they cried, what crime had they committed? As I took down their stories I could not hold back my tears either, I wept to see these poor defenceless souls, who had suffered such horrors. They were people for whom poverty was no stranger, without luxuries, who had just been trying to eke out a meagre existence. It was an appalling experience.

I contacted the newsroom of a London evening newspaper with this story and offered them the videotapes and written statements as evidence of the attack on Torjanci. A young woman journalist spent several days on the telephone with me taking down the details and the witness statements. She told me that the article would be published on a particular date. That day came and went and when I contacted her to ask why it had not been released, she said her editor had blocked it. To my knowledge, no one was ever brought to justice for this crime and there seems no record of any investigations. This, despite countless attempts to bring it to the attention of the War Crimes Tribunal in the Hague and still nothing seems to have happened.

I took statements from those who had endured torture at the hands of Tudjman's forces. There were others who asked me to write down horrifying accounts of how they had been hounded from their Croatian homes. They all had something in common. They wanted justice. They thought that I would be able to present their accounts to the U.N. or to a sympathetic public in Europe or America. It did not happen. When I did give a written account based on the statement of the Virovitisa victim, it could not be entered as evidence. This victim had been a local politician in the Serbian Democratic Party in Virovitisa in Croatia. In July of 1991, he was arrested, beaten, tortured and finally shot in the back of the head. Fortunately, the bullet entered his neck and he managed to crawl to freedom. He eventually reached Sombor in Serbia. All these victims were pathetically sure that once 'the West' knew what had happened to them, justice would prevail. After 'the West' had enforced their peace deal with Croatia and Serbia, these people were urged to return to Croatia and reclaim their homes and lives. Ludicrous though this was to expect them to go back to the place they had fled from in terror, in fear of their lives, to face an unrepentant nation again.

Occasionally people would knock on our door and ask Ilija for help. Sometimes a simple solution came from my stack of donated paracetamol and other simple remedies, none of which were readily available locally. If the medical problem was serious, there were few ways in which we could help. It always involved the lack of availability of even the most simple drugs. Later in May of 1992, a woman from the town of Darda had recently had a mastectomy in Serbia. Returning to be reunited with her family in Beli Manastir, she could not obtain the medication prescribed by her consultant and came to us for a solution. Through the extreme kindness of the U.N. Pakistan Battalion stationed in Darda, she received a regular supply of her medication. I have never forgotten what the battalion doctor said after he had promised the woman he would help if at all possible. 'We do not have this product available for most our own people in Pakistan, but I will do what I can.' True to his word he did. Unlike the Belgian battalion, the Pakistanis were popular and friendly towards the local population. Even though, they had a dreadful reputation amongst the locals as drivers. A truck being driven full pelt down the middle of the road usually heralded their arrival. It was a source of some amusement to the locals as they kept count of the number of wrecked, white trucks bearing a U.N. insignia.

Another journey, I was asked to make, was to go and film some of the damage to houses in Bilje caused by shelling from Croatia. We had to pass through the town of Darda on our way there and as we stopped at a checkpoint, we were ordered to leave our car. The policemen asked us to accompany them to the Police headquarters. We were shown into the office of Police Chief Kostich. He without any attempt at pleasantries launched into a tirade of abuse at Ilija asking him what he was doing in Darda. Ilija calmly asked him if he would like to meet me and that I was making a film for the Serbian lobby in London and had been asked by General Krstich to do it. In addition, we had a pass from the General to travel and film whatever we wanted to, where we wanted to, except for military facilities. Kostich said he didn't give a damn about General Krstich and that he decided what would happen in his district. Ilija asked why we were being detained. He answered that we weren't being detained, we were free to return to Beli Manastir and should not return to Darda. Furthermore, we were not to film anything and so we left!

I now got involved in some unusual household chores. Ilija had asked me to make him a type of sleeveless jacket with pockets that would hold a first-aid kit and a small amount of food. Other pockets were for extra ammunition clips and grenades. Having made Ilija's some of his friend's asked if I could make them one too. I eventually made eight from the ground sheets and small rucksacks they provided. One afternoon as I sewed these jackets my mother called me on our newly restored telephone line. After we had greeted each other and chatted and exchanged our news, she asked me what I was doing. 'Sewing something for Ilija,' I replied. 'How lovely dear, what are you making?' she enquired. 'A jacket with lots of pockets' said I. What I didn't tell her was that, when she called, I had been measuring a hand grenade to assess the pocket size.

CHAPTER THIRTEEN

Ilija complained bitterly about the food they were being supplied with while they were on duty guarding the frontline. Much of the salami was old and smelled awful and he was afraid they would all get food poisoning. We didn't have many options at home to supply our men with nourishing meals. The electricity was intermittent and, therefore, fridges and freezers were not working. I had plenty of potatoes and smoked, streaky bacon, some eggs, and flour. I set about making potato cakes, using mashed potato, chopped bacon, flour and egg to bind them and made around two hundred and fifty! I had arranged to meet Ilija at the last checkpoint before the front line and set off in our car to deliver the food. The morning was bright and beautiful with no frosts, it looked as if an early Spring was on its way. There were no other cars on the roads I was travelling towards Majske Medje, a small village near the River Drava and the Hungarian border. I didn't actually know where I was, in relation to the front line, and wondered whether I should have brought my passport in case I met unfriendly forces. I hoped that the area wasn't being shelled because there was very little cover.

After about a forty minutes, I came to the checkpoint at the edge of the camp and one of the men ran off to find Ilija. He took me to sit by their campfire and I met some of the men, had a look at their sleeping accommodation and it was almost time to leave. Suddenly Ilija went to the far end of their hut and came back with a tiny ginger kitten. Its little pads were scorched and burned as were its ears and whiskers. One of the men had suffered a nervous breakdown the previous night and had picked up the little kitten that had been begging food from the men and had hurled it towards the fire. One of the men quickly rescued it and some of them tried to help it by putting pig fat on its burns. The man was taken to Sombor Hospital and Ilija asked me to take the kitten home to care for. He travelled on my lap all the way back and purred the whole time. His most worrying injuries were his pads and the tips of his little ears which were raw. There were no veterinary services available for small animals at this time and so I applied antiseptic creams and lots of cuddles. We called him Ushi, meaning ears and he eventually recovered well enough to be able to walk and play, but could never climb very well. I think his ability to extend his claws had been compromised. We could never keep our animals very long, they became so terrified of the shelling they would run and hide and some just never came back. Ushi was with us for about 2 years before disappearing. I never gave up hope that he had found a home with better food. Cats can be like that sometimes, especially if a dog moves into their domain and we were later to take in two.

The children were profoundly affected by these dramatic changes to their lives. The younger ones, by the nightly interruptions to their slumbers and some of the older boys who, without their fathers around became unruly. One of our neighbour's sons Joko was always up for a challenge and when one of his friends bragged about his shooting prowess, he promptly challenged him to a contest. He took one of his father's hunting rifles and ammunition and set off to meet his fellow competitors. They were all aged around eleven or twelve. Casually emerging from his front door, rifle slung over his shoulder, Joko was immediately spotted by Ilija, who was enjoying a day off. Ilija sprinted across the road to him and asked what he was doing. Choosing his words very carefully, Joko told Ilija that he was going to test the gun. He got no further with his explanation as Ilija promptly disarmed him and relieved him of the ammunition. He kept it all until Joko's father returned home from his tour of duty. He was very grateful and instructed Ilija to put Joko over his knee for a good hiding if he caught him again. Ilija did catch him again, this time strolling along on his way to school with a regular army TT 7.62 pistol tucked into his belt. Taking him by the back of his neck Ilija shook him, relieved him of the gun and took him home. Fortunately, Joko saw the error of his ways. However, about this time a neighbour suffered a dreadful tragedy which affected everyone very deeply and not just those living nearby. The Police, Special Police Forces, and RSK Territorials all had their regular issue ammunition supplies, stored in their homes. Most were extremely careful about storing these munitions. Sadly, one neighbour made a tragic mistake with terrible consequences. He had two young sons aged 6 and 8 years old and returning from a weeks tour of duty he dropped his spare ammunition haversack just inside the doorway of his home. His wife was at work and the children's grandmother was minding the children. He went to bed, forgetting to put away the haversack. The boys took a grenade from it and began to play with it in their garden. Both boys were killed when the grenade exploded.

And so it continued, everyone grimly 'trying to make the best of it'. I had decided to make some doughnuts to share with some friends on my birthday in March. I made the dough, quite a large amount of it so that Ilija could take some doughnuts back with him to share with his friends on duty. I left it piled in the middle of the table, about a 3 kg, covered it with a cloth and decided to go to my neighbour's house for the ritual drinking of Turkish coffee. I love this coffee, thick, strong and sweet I used to joke that it was my morning fix! Although it is referred to as Turkish, the reason is entirely different to what, you the reader, may imagine. It is not drunk like this in Turkey but, was given the name because, during the occupation of Serbia by the Ottomans, the Turks were the only people who could afford to drink real coffee. Those living under the occupation drank ersatz coffee made from herbs and roots. I once made this Turkish coffee for my father to try. Although I warned him against draining the cup to the dregs, he forgot and an agonized expression came across his face as he felt the coffee grounds. He rushed to spit them into some kitchen towel and then said 'God! That's horrible! Don't they have proper coffee there?' Now as I sat with my friends, waiting for the doughnut dough that I had left on the table at home to rise, the alarm sounded. We all headed for the basement. During these times, no one ever left their home without turning all the appliances off in the event of an attack and so no one had any safety concerns. This was one of the longest attacks I had experienced in the whole time I was there and it was to be some 12 hours later before I could safely return home. We had got used to the stop – start nature of the attacks and had to wait until we were entirely sure it was over. At home, I was greeted by the sight of a mass of dough. The yeast had done its job and now the top of the table was entirely covered and it was hanging down over the edge. It was rock-hard. I groaned inwardly realising that due to the length of the raid the water had been turned off and probably wouldn't be turned on again until morning. I scraped off as much as I could but, eventually gave up and went to bed. The waste of so many precious ingredients was the worst part of it all.

A regular visitor to our shelter was a large, shaggy dog, as large as an Irish Wolfhound. He was a Serbian Sharplanina or shepherd dog from a nearby house. As soon as the shelling began his owners would let him run free because he howled in terror as the shells landed. One night he came to me as I was waiting to enter the shelter and so I petted him, took him by the collar and led him down into the basement. There were shouts of protest from some of the women who demanded that he be turned out in case he bit the little children. I agreed to keep him close by me and promised to hold him close to me all the time. They agreed to this, but unluckily for me the dog stank. He smelled so awful my eyes were running but, he was a sweet dog and always stayed quietly by my side. That experience was repeated for several attacks until very sadly, one night, he was killed outright by one of the falling shells.

During March of 1992, the shelling of Beli Manastir had become worse and worse. There was intermittent shelling doing daylight hours and then early evening. Just when everyone thought it had ended and finally put their exhausted children to bed, it would suddenly start again around nine or ten in the evening. Sometimes this would be over within the half-hour, and the people would emerge from their shelter and return to bed. Then roused again, around 2 a.m by sirens or more explosions, everyone jumped quickly out of bed and ran again to the shelters. Eventually one night after several such episodes, I was so exhausted that I just rolled out of bed onto the floor. Pulling my pillow and duvet from the bed, I went back to sleep to the sound of shells crashing around us outside. Oblivious to it all, I slept until late into the morning! I had begun to have nightmares at this time. Poor Ilija! One night I leapt out of bed telling him that there were red hot pieces of a bomb in the bed. He shook me gently and pointed to a hair clip I had been lying on!

By far my worst nightmare began to happen more frequently. In a strange state somewhere between sleep and wakefulness, needing to go to the bathroom, I put my foot out of bed. But I couldn't feel the floor. Quickly withdrawing it, I sat in terror for a few minutes until I became fully conscious and was able to reason that there must be a floor! I sometimes shook Ilija to tell him the floor had gone, but as I said the words I would add, 'it's ok I think I am dreaming again.' He was endlessly kind and gentle and would hug me tightly telling me to lie down and go to sleep. Sometimes I struggled to get free because I wanted to go to the bathroom, and he thought I was sleep walking! By far the worst times were when I was alone in the house, I hated it and usually didn't sleep much. I had developed different ways of behaving during the shelling. When it was dark, I usually went to my neighbour's basement and had a special bag packed because it was hard to know how long I would be there. Carrying all my jewellery, passport and papers, precious photographs, medications, my knitting and Ilija's guitar. If I was alone, it was quite an undertaking! During the daytime, it was easier to judge how far away the shells were landing, whether in Beli Manastir or surrounding villages. If it were the latter I, stayed at home and continued with my chores and singing all the hymns I had ever learnt, by heart, very loudly. If it got a little closer, I would retreat to the wood store and chop wood, which also got rid of much nervous energy.

Most of the women were extremely courageous, they were trying to care for their children, much of the time without electricity and enduring water rationing. Food shortages and scarcity also made their lives so much harder. Some relief came from some Red Cross supplies they could sometimes buy from refugees. Dried milk powder was the most prized purchase next to washing powder. Chocolate was made as a special treat for the children from the milk powder, for it had been a long time since the shops had stocks of sweets and chocolate. I even learned how to boil white fabrics in clean wood ash which made it remarkably white! We were very fortunate to have a family living in the village with livestock and once a month we received staples such as potatoes, beans, eggs, milk and cheese and some smoked meat. We often shared this with others who had no family with farming connections. But this was unremarkable because everyone shared.

It was the beginning of March and had been snowing for most of the day. In the evening, I heard the sound of distant artillery and Ilija went outside to look around. He returned and asked me to don my ski suit and to bring my shopping bag of treasures with me, just in case. I followed him outside. We made our way through the snow drifts to the end of the street and watched as the distant sky over the village of Jagonjak was lit with the flashes of tanks shells. We watched in silence, I wondered if Vida and her neighbours were being targeted, Ilija said that perhaps the barrage heralded an attack. There was a dreadful beauty to this awful light display and neither of us spoke as we huddled together. I have always suffered from a most embarrassing problem. If ever I go for hikes, walks in the forest or anywhere else where there isn't a lavatory immediately available I always feel the need to use one. Airline stewardesses wheeling food trolleys along the walkway on a plane also has the same effect. I was once holidaying on a cruise ship which anchored off Dakar in Senegal. We were to spend the day ashore but were advised to use the ships lavatories and a boat would be available all day to run a ferry service. I think I spent more time on that boat than in Dakar.

This night hunkered down in a snow-filled ditch in my ski suit was no exception. The suit usually got so hot after a while that I only wore a bra and pants under it. Some of the shells were now landing in Beli Manastir and so I either had to make a dash for the shelter or strip off my suit and go in the ditch. I stripped off. Within seconds, as luck would have it, one of the jeeps carrying some of Ilija's unit arrived to collect him, before I could get back into the ski suit. There was applause for what they assumed were two hardy lovers in the ditch. Explanations were useless Ilija accepted their admiration, bade me farewell and hopped into the jeep while I made my way to the shelter. I like to think that my ratings in the 'hot' stakes went up after that!

As the conditions hardened, I decided to start sending telegrams to the head of the UN Boutrous Boutrous-Ghali. We had heard that the UN would move into the area and put an end to the shelling from Osijek so that peace talks could take place. There were UN troops who had arrived in Baranja and some had taken over the old Yugoslavian Army barracks on the outskirts of Beli Manastir.when the J.N.A were forced to withdraw to Serbia. The UN troops were Belgians and behaved very strangely. Once they moved into the old Yugoslavian Army barracks, they immediately sandbagged the perimeter and set up what looked like machine gun emplacements. At first, the inhabitants of the town were a little fearful of this aberration as they passed by. However, gradually the Belgians hunkered down behind their sandbags became a source of amusement and derision. They appeared menacing, something the populace had not expected for they had waited to welcome them as protectors. Several telegrams later, around the 25th March 1992. Ilija and I received a visit from two Officers of the Belgian Army. They told me that although I was claiming in these telegrams that frequent incursions were being made into the territory of Baranja by Croatian forces, in fact, they had not witnessed any such incidents. I replied that they could hardly observe any incursions happening all along the front lines, some 7 km away at the closest point to them, when they were sitting behind their sandbags in their barracks. Now he affirmed that since he had not witnessed any attacks he could not report them. And he was not allowed to go and patrol that area until the mandate had been passed by the UN security council. I was later to see a report he sent to the UN headquarters that the UN barracks in Beli Manastir had been hit by Artillery fire. The same barrage was falling on the town too, but he didn't attribute the blame for the attack to Croatia.

He now asked me to give the undertaking to stop sending telegrams to Boutrous Boutrous- Ghali because this was causing problems. Of course, I said I could not give them any such undertaking. Everyone knew even if they didn't, that all the signs indicated that very shortly Baranja would be attacked by the Croatian Army and the people were very frightened. Ilija told them how he and the others protecting the front line had seen a massive build-up of Croatian forces on the opposite side of the River Drava. And moreover, that there were many groups of Croats moving into Baranja all along the front line. All they could reply was that they had not seen it and they were not allowed to report what they had not seen.I told him how my Croatian neighbour had warned me that it would happen and that their forces would kill anyone they found. Our plan was to hide in the Cornfield or try to make it to their UN barracks. They left without any resolution and I really wondered why they had come. Eventually, I found out that they had been ordered to visit me and explain the current position of the UN. Their stance had been ludicrous, equally as ludicrous, as their claim to not know what was happening regarding the planned attack. Were we to believe they did not have access to satellite and other intelligence? I had trusted the UN forces up to this encounter. I assumed they were on the side of right and would protect civilians. Claims as to their bias I had privately dismissed as paranoia. Now I doubted their integrity.

Everyone felt strongly that the UN was not going to help prevent any Croatian Army attack on the civilians in Baranja. That the Croatians had a window of opportunity to attack and retake Baranja before the UN resolution vote designated to be held on 7TH April 1992. This attack, if successful would save the UN the problem of resolving the situation that existed in the area. Only our local men with the help of the territorial conscripts in the Krajina Army could or would protect the inhabitants because the UN would not and the Yugoslavian Army had been forced to leave. We now made some plans as to what we would do in the event of such an attack. I had a coffee mug with a British flag on it and for one crazy moment thought that I could bring all the families from our street into our home. I would then approach any Croat soldiers with my mug in hand to explain I was British and they were my family. Almost to a person, the refugees, and even the locals believed that if the Croatian soldiers broke through our lines, they would slaughter people as they had in the Serbian villages in Croatia the previous year. I had to make a more realistic plan than that!

The plan now was to try and get to the UN barracks a couple of kilometres away. We discussed how many cars and drivers we had amongst the women neighbours, for the men would all be required on the front line. We organized which cars would be used for children and which for the elderly and others. We didn't have enough drivers. How many cars could another car with a driver tow behind them? Did we have any tow ropes? Could we teach anyone to drive by just showing them how to steer and where the brake pedal was? We also urged the women to pack their valuables to take with them but only in small bags because there would be no room for large bags or boxes.

We were all in a state of nervous anticipation and dread. I went, as usual, to share a morning coffee with my friend Dushanka. Almost as soon as I had sat down at her table, she asked me to do her favour. 'Of course, what is it?' I said. 'Give me a cigarette,' came her reply. I reached for my cigarettes and handed her the packet saying, 'but you don't smoke?' 'Never mind,' said she lighting it and immediately puffing like mad on it. After a few minutes, she put it down in the ashtray, a look of disappointment crossing her face. 'Nothing, it hasn't helped me calm down at at all.' I began to laugh which just made her frown. 'Well, you always say it relaxes you and so does Dusan (her husband). No damn good at all!' I did try to explain that people inhale to get some sort of benefit from smoking and puffing on it like she did really was pointless. And so that was the morning Dushanka took up smoking and gave up smoking all before we had drunk our first coffee of the day.

I awoke to the sound of our telephone ringing early in the morning around four a.m on the 3rd April 1992. To my surprise as I stumbled towards the source of this irritating noise I saw Ilija fully-dressed in his combat uniform. I stood there in my dressing gown as he told me that a large attack had started and he had about twenty minutes and then he would have to leave. I cut up some bread and pieces of smoked bacon and putting them into a plastic bag, pushed them into a little corner of his backpack. Typically, he would only take a bag of dried fruit, nuts and chocolate. He said this instant source of energy was the most practical because it didn't make him thirsty. Most of the men in our sector had expected an attack. Over the previous ten days, their patrols had seen a great deal of activity on the Croatian side of the River Drava. And there had also been many more incursions by Croatian forces than usual, into the swamps and forest bordering Kopachski Rit. The shelling had become more intensive and many, like Ilija, hadn't slept well, expecting the attack to begin at any time. Now, having been alerted by the telephone calls, gathering their ammunition, backpacks, and a little food the men emerged from their houses, weapons slung over their shoulders. Ilija held me very close and we hugged each other tightly. He said that if a second siren were heard that was the signal that their positions had been overrun. I should take as many children and the elderly as possible in our car and go as fast as I could to the UN base. From there we would probably be evacuated to Serbia once it was safe to do so. If he survived, we would find each other in Sombor, Serbia. I heard the first sirens resounding over the town. Following him to the front door and kissing him goodbye waving to the others in the jeeps and watching the other men in the street running towards their designated areas. I went immediately to fetch a bucket of water to throw down the steps of the house after he had left, something many of the wives did. It was meant to somehow protect him and is a very, old tradition. And I sobbed uncontrollably.

After the men had gone and the sirens stopped a stillness settled over everything. All the women gradually gathered together, I felt numb as I think did they, for none of us talked for a while. Someone suggested we all went to their house and drink some coffee together and plan what we were to do. Those without little children to tend went to sit with the other women. Finally, we decided to go back to our homes and collect what we could, ready to leave at a moment's notice. I soon finished my packing and went to see how Dushanka was coping. I found her wandering from room to room. She was sobbing and told me she couldn't decide what to take or what to leave. She had lived here for the past thirty years since her marriage to Dusan and didn't know where to begin. People made the strangest decisions, brought on by shock I think. Some women were cleaning their windows, polishing, and dusting, saying they didn't want the Croatians to think them, bad housewives. Others were packing only old clothes or cutlery, leaving their best and newest possessions or silverware behind. They were worried about losing them or damaging what they took.

We tried to support one another as best we could and I admired their resilience and an air of stoicism that allowed the daily routine to continue. It would have been very easy to give way to despair or panic. I hoped to get all the small bags of my neighbours into the boot of our car, a Fiat Argenta. This car had literally been in the wars! Its windscreen was peppered with bullet holes, scars from an unsuccessful ambush by Croatian paramilitaries at the end of July. Ilija had been en route to visit his mother in Jagodnjak and had had a lucky escape. I can not recall, in any detail, what I did for the rest of that day. I seemed to drift through it, at times praying, at times singing my repertoire of hymns: abide with me, the twenty-third psalm and others I could recall. For I believe in the power of prayer and it helped me to focus on practical matters. There was a lot of coffee drunk, probably many cigarettes smoked and the children were kept indoors. The oldest were aware of what they had to do in the event of an alarm sounding. I do recall that to a woman we were listening for the wail of sirens. The signal to run.

I was to hear from Ilija, but days later, how events unfolded on that day in April of 1992. Ilija's unit of 13 army Pioneers drove towards the forward positions in their sector, close to a point called Vila Lock where the water levels of the channels of the River Drava were controlled. The other Pioneer groups spread out into the other sectors of the front line with orders to regroup the Territorials holding those positions and generally reorganize the defence until the Command headquarters could send in more reinforcements. They had been told that the Croatians were breaking through all along the front. They had crossed the River Drava, probably a few days before and hidden in the forests of an area of no man's land which stretched from the banks of the river up to the Serbian front line. At around 6.40 a.m Ilija's group advanced, with great caution, towards Vila Lock. They were unsure of how many Croatians had managed to break through in their area and therefore, what they would find at the Lock. The forest was sometimes dense sometimes sparser. However, the Pioneers knew the area very well and using the forest as cover came within 500 metres or so of the buildings there, which had served as their barracks in that sector. Now they saw small groups of their Territorials running towards them. They were panic stricken saying that they had lost at least fifteen of their number and that the Croats had overrun their defensive positions and were now in control of the buildings ahead. They managed to calm the men telling them that if they ran, their families would be in mortal danger and that they should return with them. These Territorials were farmers, not soldiers and were filled with horror at what they had seen. Bravely, they agreed to go back with the Pioneers and try to retake the position. Around 7 a.m after regrouping the unit now totalled 30 men and they advanced towards Vila Lock under cover of the trees and undergrowth. A fierce firefight began and lasted around twenty minutes until finally the Croatians began to retreat back to an area of no man's land, towards the Drava. After the unit had recaptured Vila Lock, they used their field telephones to report to the R.S.K. Command centre at Majske Medje. It was North-West of Beli Manastir close to the Hungarian border. They urgently requested reinforcements and the Command reply was that they would send help as soon as they could but, in the meantime, they must hold that position at all costs. And that the front line had been compromised at many points. When the alarm had been sent out at 7 a.m., several thousand Serbian reinforcements had been ordered to gather in Beli Manastir, as the Command brought in all the reserve units stationed around Baranja. These men were the people of Baranja and some of the refugees from Croatia, who had settled there. They fought fiercely to defend what they believed was their sacred land. Many Serbian people do regard their land as sacred and they do not differ from many other countries like Russia and the USA in this belief.

These reinforcements now swung the battle firmly in favour of the Serbian forces and they began to push the Croatians back towards the Drava.

At Vila Lock, after several smaller attacks by the Croats, a larger attack was mounted at around 11 a.m. By now Ilija's group had lost 13 men killed or wounded and it had taken four hours of desperate defence before the reinforcements finally made it to their sector. The Pioneers and Territorials were now endeavouring to strengthen their lines by linking up with the other groups and by midday they had succeeded in stabilizing the entire front line and forced the Croats to retreat.

A last desperate attack was launched by the Croats at around 12.30 p.m when the Croatian forces brought small armoured cars and tanks that they had ferried across the Drava using a pontoon bridge. They drove along the forest service road with loudspeakers mounted on the vehicles playing strident military marching music. As they advanced, they fired bursts from their machine guns mounted on the turrets.This attack was a disastrous decision on the part of their commanders, because there was only one, single-track service road through this forest and swamp land and they were easy targets. A lone pioneer, dug-in by this track destroyed the first two armoured cars using an 82 mm M60 anti-tank gun. The remaining 8 or 9 of the tanks and vehicles could not pass and their crews panicked and abandoned them, running back towards their lines in full retreat. All around machine guns were firing from both sides and there was mayhem. Many of the Croats had been killed or wounded. Further, down the lines, all that day wave after wave of Croats were trying to break through this 12 km front line and were repulsed by its defenders.

The dead and wounded from both sides lay where they had fallen. It was almost impossible to calculate just how many had died or been wounded, especially the Croatians. Some of their men drowned as they tried to cross the River Drava back to Croatia. The remains of others were sometimes discovered by Serbian patrols in the forests around the battleground for many months to come. Some had been partially eaten by wildlife. Estimates of Serbian losses were around 30 killed and a similar number wounded. These were also the numbers quoted from Croatian sources regarding their losses. However, it was impossible to confirm these figures.

A dreadful indictment against the leaders of the Croatian army would be the extreme youth of their soldiers, inexperience, lack of training, without any direction and very probably that many of them were taking drugs. Their behaviour was judged by the Serbian soldiers to be crazily erratic. They would scream and fire their weapons until all their ammunition was exhausted and then drop their weapons and run. Evidence of drug taking amongst these men was found on some of the corpses and wounded and it included, syringes, ampules, powder, and tablets. Ilija was horrified and related that he had seen 5 of the Croats with these drugs in their pockets. The Pioneers now advanced towards the River Drava to check that all the Croatians had left. Gradually the firing ceased until at around 3 p.m everything was over.

Ilija said that there was no sense of euphoria after this victory. They felt that they had saved Baranja but were sickened by the casualties. Ilija and I never discussed this battle. I heard from various people accounts of what had happened and when I decided to write this book I asked him to tell me what he could remember of that day. And so we have tried to describe it without embellishment and as truthfully as he can recall after such a long time. He was so deeply affected by the images of that day that he has always found it difficult to revisit the experience.

Meanwhile, in Beli Manastir, as the day wore on without any news we waited, afraid because we had no news and yet fearing it too. In the late afternoon, one of my neighbours ran out of her house yelling and whooping. It was alright, our lines had held and the Croatians were in full retreat. She had been watching a local television station and had actually seen her husband and his unit making their way back to Beli Manastir. We gathered around her and she named those that she had seen. Ilija wasn't one of them because he was in a different group. Then she urged me to go with her to the town centre to await the arrival of the trucks bringing the dead and wounded back to the medical centre. I didn't go. I just couldn't face the spectacle of the wives and mothers trying to catch a glimpse of the dead and wounded, searching for their loved ones amongst the casualties. Eventually, I got a call from one of our friends that Ilija was safe and unhurt. He was now translating for a group of around nine or ten UN and European monitors who had arrived at their forward position on the frontline.

Incredibly, although the attack had been launched from Croatia at around 4 a.m that morning and fierce fighting had raged all day along the whole 12 km perimeter, there was no response from the UN forces. After the Croatians had retreated and the fighting had ended some eleven hours later, they appeared on the front lines. Ilija was asked by one of his officers to accompany the group along the perimeter and translate the conversations they wanted to have with other randomly chosen members of the units that had been involved in the battle. The UN battalion had spent their whole day in their barracks in Beli Manastir. Their mandate, they said, did not allow them to take any steps to intervene until the 6th April 1992. Neither to make any moves to avert the battle nor to protect the Serbian civilian population in the towns and villages in the event of a Croatian break through.

They now asked different groups to explain what had taken place, what they had witnessed. They also asked for casualty figures. They carefully wrote down all the answers they received. All the casualties from both sides were collected by the Territorials, loaded into lorries and driven to Beli Manastir. From there the wounded were taken to Sombor Hospital in Serbia. None of the soldiers could get permission to go and visit their comrades in Sombor Hospital and therefore, Ilija was delighted when we were given the opportunity to visit them.

CHAPTER FOURTEEN

On the fifth of April Ilija and I were summoned to a meeting in Knezevi Vinogradi, a town, about 8 miles from Beli Manastir on the road to the Batina Bridge crossing into Serbia. At the meeting were UN officers from Belbat and civilian EU monitors. General Krstich of the J.N.A, Commanding General of all the troops in Baranja and several other high ranking J.N.A officers. Ilija received a telephone call that morning informing him that he was the appointed translator at an important meeting in Knezevi Vinogradi and would he, please bring me along too. These requests had come from General Krstich. An army staff car arrived and drove us to the meeting. All that remains as a memory of this meeting is one incident involving me and a Belgian UN Officer and the copious amounts of alcohol being consumed. Ilija has no recollection at all of the conversations that took place. Probably because he was exhausted after the events of the previous 48 hours.

I, on the other hand, remember perfectly well that the Belgian UN officer leant towards me and said conspiratorially 'You see Amanda, you don't understand. These Serbs do not live in the type of cultured society as you and I do and so you can not expect them to behave in the same civilised way as us.' Neither Ilija nor I were ever certain of exactly how much the General or his staff understood English. However, after this meeting General Krstich told Ilija that his door was always open to he and I should we need his help in the future. This generous offer came after I had made my reply to the Belgian Officer's remark about the Serbs. Which was 'I am astounded that the UN choose such ill-educated officers to serve in a country that they are so very obviously ignorant of. Serbian culture dates from at least the 7th Century unlike I believe Belgium which is what? 200 years old?' I thought it appalling that this person should make such a remark in earshot of these Serbian Army Officers. All the more dreadful because he believed they didn't speak or understand English. Or, he didn't care.

Ilija was now asked to accompany the EU monitors to visit the wounded from the battle of the 3rd April, who were in Sombor Hospital across the Batina Bridge inside Serbia. He was in great demand as a translator because there were so few available, at this time, with the necessary level of fluency in both Serbian and English languages. The monitors travelled in their car and we shared a J.N.A staff car with a lieutenant driver and a Colonel whom we had never met before. As we drove towards Sombor, I was blithely enjoying the scenery when I became aware of Ilija suddenly becoming very tense and was clearly furiously angry at something the driver had said. Ilija turned to me saying that the officer had said that things would be much better now, because the murderous and thieving, Police Special Forces units had been disbanded. Choking with rage Ilija told him to stop the car because he had been a member of this group who had, in fact, tried hard to prevent the lootings and killings in Baranja. And, what's more, some J.N.A army officers had been heavily involved with the criminal gangs there. The car screeched to a halt and the incongruity of the prospect of Ilija and this army officer fighting on the highway made me gasp. The colonel swiftly took command ordering the lieutenant to stay where he was and continue driving us to Sombor. He turned to Ilija and asked him to be calm and apologized for any offence that had been caused. We continued without incident. Ilija duly accompanied the EU representatives and was able to see all his friends and carry messages to them from their loved ones.

As we left the hospital, our staff car awaited us and to my horror, I saw that we had the same driver but without the colonel. I had reckoned without the vagaries of the Serbian male. The lieutenant embraced Ilija, explaining that he had just repeated what he had heard and he was deeply sorry because his colonel had told him otherwise. Ilija sat next to him now and I sat in the rear. They were now talking about past events like old friends. I was trying to resist the urge to sleep when Ilija turned and said 'Oh, by the way, the officer says that there have been reports of sniper fire all along this road and so you might like to lie down until we reach Beli Manastir.' My immediate thought as usual of, thank you, Lord, that my mother can't see me, flashed through my brain as I lay down. Dusk was now falling rapidly and we drove at break-neck speed arriving safely at our home about half an hour later. Ilija now contacted all the families of the men he had seen which was of great comfort to the families who could not go to Sombor themselves. At this time, no one was allowed to leave Baranja without special permission.

Gradually over the next few weeks, the UN began to make their presence felt in the area. After their mandate had been implemented on the 7th April, there was no more shelling of the area by the Croatians. However, the front line was still being held by the Pioneers and Territorials and the Croats were still entering Baranja and the occasional firefights continued. Belbat, the Belgian UN contingent took up positions just behind no-mans-land in May 1992. However since no one trusted them, the Pioneers and Territorials continued with their patrols and defensive positions. We heard about peace initiatives, but no one had a clear idea of what lay ahead for them.

I was now able to travel to visit my family in England. I boarded one of the last few Yugoslavian Airlines flights because sanctions were to be imposed within the coming weeks preventing YAT airline from overflying other countries. Many people could not obtain visas now for the U.K. and other European destinations and so the airport was almost empty, with few staff or passengers. There were three of us at the departure gate waiting to board the aircraft and as we boarded the stewardess pointed us to the first three seats, on the left, in the economy section. My fellow travellers, a large elderly man and his equally large wife and I sat squashed together, listening to the stewardess as she gave us the safety instructions. Once airborne

I called her over and asked if we might sit in one of the other free seats. Rather grudgingly, she told us that we may, but we were not to go to the back of the plane, please. I really didn't blame her for that, since it would have made her job much harder had we all done so! On a previous flight, I had been seated next to a relief pilot and I was invited into the cockpit to look at the lights of Munich as we flew over. I don't like heights, but not wanting to appear churlish I smiled and looked down to where he was pointing. I smiled my thanks and fled back to my seat, it was such a strange sensation to see nothing ahead but the clouds. I could never pilot a plane and am full of admiration for those that can!

On my return to Coventry, I was advised that Srbo Krnjulac and other members of the Serbian expatriate community were working with my mother to collect aid for Baranja. Srbo was an amazing man. Well, into his eighties he would always cycle over to see me from his home on the other side of Coventry, whenever he had some news for me. Like so many of his friends who had arrived in the UK seeking asylum from the Communist regime in Yugoslavia, he had never forgotten his beloved Serbia. He and others, over several years, built the Serbian Orthodox Church in Birmingham. They toiled every weekend on their days off from their regular jobs. There were poignant reminders of a distant homeland that he and his friends obviously missed so very much. I attended several of their slavas where their British wives had tried to produce Serbian specialities, from food bought at the local supermarket. Valiant attempts, but a pale reflection of the original dishes. They attempted to keep up these traditional celebrations of slava and fasting. Of the marking of important dates on their Orthodox religious calendar. Srbo had been training as a monk but, left this life to fight for his country when it was attacked by Hitler and his Nazi allies the Croatians. He had escaped through Italy after Churchill abandoned the Cetnik Royalist side to support Tito and the Communists. To stay would probably have meant death for these men and so they came to Britain. Most of them had married British women and their offspring were raised as British. Many of the wives and children did not learn to speak

Serbian and it must have been difficult to resist adopting December 25th as their Christmas Day. Who could fail to be swept along with all the expectation and excitement surrounding them?

I detected a certain irritation on the part of some of the wives, resentful that their households were the poorer for the amount of money their spouses spent on Serbian causes. Srbo's love for his country shone like a beacon and I was often moved to tears by this simple man's dedication. He used to call me his little Serbian fighter laughing uproariously as he said it. I didn't truly understand his profound dilemma and the longing he had for his homeland and family he had left so abruptly until many years later.

My situation was by choice unlike Srbo and I gradually adapted to my life in Serbia. I usually travelled to be with my family in the UK for Christmas and Easter and continued to visit every couple of months. I slipped gradually into a way of life that meant I could feel comfortable in either society. I can move freely between my two homes which he could not. However, I tried hard to adapt and become part of this new community. Of course, our view of ourselves is not as others see us! When in later years, as I imagined myself to be outwardly, at least, a 'local' and was teaching English in a local Valjevo private school, one of my colleagues giggled as I drew my handkerchief from where it was tucked up my sleeve. And I am always reprimanded for putting my handbag on the floor, appalling luck here! I am comfortable now, however, living in either country for we wives are mostly the same. What to cook for lunch? Hatred of cleaning windows or ironing? And in my case, hatred of housework, in particular. I try hard to respect traditions and beliefs and keep quiet if I disagree with them. I respect my country of choice while I love my country of birth. I know this when tears spring spontaneously if I watch 'The last night of the Proms.' Joining in with the rendition of Rule Britannia! I don't approve at all of the lyrics but the memories it evokes of warm days watching cricket or tennis makes me homesick! Ilija pulls dreadful faces at me as I roar back at him the lines, 'Britannia rules the waves, Britains never, never, never shall be slaves!' The hardest times are when England and Serbia are playing a football match. Or when

Djokovic plays tennis against Andy Murray. But after all, Murray is Scottish and so I support Djokovic!

My Mother's church, St. Margarets in Coventry, was the base for the Aid for Baranja operation and eventually over 250 boxes of aid donated by British Serbs besides many other kind people were shipped. We seemed to be missing out on any other relief supplies there. I had spoken to Prince Tomislav about it, but he and his wife were doing their part, buying and ferrying ambulances to Bosnia. I knew that Serbs from all over the World were sending donations, but these funds were, I was told, all being managed by the Serbian Orthodox Church. I contacted them, but they were not interested in helping Baranja. Many people helped along the way in the transporting of our aid, including Y.A.T (Yugoslav Airlines). They were simply marvellous and always allowed my nearly 100 kg of luggage when I flew back carrying relief supplies in my luggage. And they flew the larger shipments of aid free of charge and arranged for its safe storage at Belgrade airport until it could be collected. The customs control also cleared it and, therefore, there were no customs charges levied. A good friend from Shepherd's Bush in London had arranged free transportation from Coventry to Heathrow Airport and there was also free transport from Belgrade to Baranja. The next group that stepped up to help were the American Society of Friends. Quite unexpectedly I was contacted by this group who wanted to donate £12,000 towards providing medical supplies for the clinic in Beli Manastir, Baranja. I arranged for them to pay the money directly to a Serbian drug company called Galenica who then gave the medical centre a credit account to draw on.

Despite the desperate need amongst the populace of Baranja, the criminals were still active and were intent on stealing aid whenever the opportunity presented itself. The Red Cross centre in Beli Manastir quickly distributed the relief to all the villages. We decided to share the toys between the polyclinics for the use of their small patients. One of the worst thefts by the criminals was hundreds of gift bags of chocolate, intended for distribution amongst the children of the area. Chocolate and sweets had long been unavailable and news of the donation was greeted with tremendous joy and anticipation. Suddenly the whole consignment disappeared and enquiries were met with a shrug of the shoulders from the officials in charge of it. A relatively short while later a shop in the centre of Beli Manastir had an enormous display in its window of gift bags of chocolate. The following night there was a loud explosion that destroyed the display along with the rest of the shop. Rough, but effective justice when the local police force refuses to carry out their duty.

Life was settling into a new routine. There was no more shelling, but I saw even less of Ilija than I had before. They now had to serve ten days patrolling the front lines and then had a few hours or at most 24 hours free. This was extremely difficult for the people. The farmers were struggling to plant their crops and later to harvest them and to collect the wood for winter. Several journalists now appeared in Beli Manastir and I was interviewed by some of them. A Belgian journalist seemed sincerely interested in understanding the situation and Ilija was given time off to escort him around the area and they visited many of the villages. He saw the old Serbian Orthodox churches for himself, the graveyards and Calvinist Churches all attesting to who exactly had lived in this area for the past hundred years or so. The tombstones provided the clearest evidence of ethnicity with the names on the headstones. He accepted our offer of accommodation because there were no hotels working and the curfew was still in place preventing his departure that night and he left the following day. We later had a strange message from him telling us that his newspaper was furious with his report based on what we had shown and told him and that he may lose his job. We never heard any more from him and were deeply saddened by the reaction to what had been clear evidence to support the Serbian claims for Baranja. We had long thought the news media biased and, of course, this was reported as paranoia on our part. Because, in the world of the media, the people with the loudest voice can easily shout down those with a tiny voice. A Serbian filmmaker came and made a documentary about us. One of the benefits derived after the programme was aired on Serbian TV was that many times, as I went through passport control in Belgrade Airport, one of the officers came out and hugged me!

A horse and cart were being driven slowly along our street with the driver shouting out a message. It reminded me of the rag and bone man who used to give us balloons in return for any junk we could prise from our parents. His quest was similar but his motive entirely different. He was collecting winter clothing for the refugees especially the young male conscripts on the front line. My friend and I discussed what to do. We finally decided, in our wisdom, that as we would probably have to be evacuated quickly if there were another attack by the Croats, we may as well be generous. We were very generous with our men's warm winter coats, trousers, and socks. We had regularly donated a cutlery set,1 knife,1 fork, and one spoon as more refugees arrived and often a blanket if we could spare one. Sometimes they had collected saucepans or plates and cups, but this was the first time they had asked for clothing. As the chilly days of Autumn approached in 1992, I packed away our summer clothes. Lifting up the suitcases onto the table for me to unpack Ilija's face bore a look of astonishment when I opened the case containing his much-depleted wardrobe of winter clothing. But, true to the man I knew, he didn't complain when I explained the reason for his generosity!

Another of my household chores saw me washing the Croatian flag that had been torn down from the Police Station in Beli Manastir after the Croatian forces had withdrawn to Croatia. It had been covered in mud and thrust into a plastic bag and since I thought it to be an important trophy for Ilija and his men I worked hard to get it clean. Then I hung it outside on the washing line. About ten minutes later my neighbour and friend Dushanka telephoned me. 'Maya' she said 'for goodness sake take down that bloody flag, they are meeting to discuss whether you have changed sides!'

I have warm memories of these people that I lived amongst during this terrible time. They lived in constant fear of attack, had little or no money or, food and a bleak future. Their children made the best of it with various games and usually could be found playing in the street. Ilija had acquired some beehives and we were given two colonies and settled down to wait for the delicious honey and combs to come. Luka was the 5-year-old half- brother of one of the first casualties of the fighting in Beli Manastir, 27-year-old Ratko. After the death of his brother he was even more spoiled than before and everyone made a special fuss of him. He was a devilish child, with dancing eyes, always full of fun and always naughty! We had seen him lurking around the beehives on the wasteland behind our house and Ilija talked to him very seriously about the dangers of bees and not to go too near. All the other children knew and respected this and the hives were well away from where they played. Ilija had given them a nice talk about what the bees were making and that they would all share in the honey and combs when they were harvested. Luka did not want to wait any longer for his share. One sunny afternoon, very fortunately for him, most of the adults were also outside chatting to each other and enjoying the warmth of the day. Suddenly, we all saw Luka rush up to one of the beehives and lifting up the cover on the top of the hive he thrust his head inside the hive. Ilija yelled and ran quickly to him, grabbing him by the scruff of his neck, he threw him away from the hive before replacing the lid. Luka stood up, Ilija picked off the bees that were in his hair and we all held our breath! He began to wail and rubbing his head and arms ran, yelling at the top of his voice, to his home nearby. Ilija followed and was very relieved to find that the boy had only a couple of stings on his head and on his arms. He had been very lucky. Not that lucky, though, because his mother punished him further for his naughtiness!

We now acquired a dog. Many of the abandoned dogs had been shot to end their suffering. A few were rescued. We helped one such dog whose Serbian owners had left for Serbia. A neighbour people alerted us to the fact that there was a dog chained to his kennel in an empty property. Ilija went and cutting his chain brought him and we called him Bodger. Like a bodge up, something made but not very expertly. He was obviously a senior of the canine world. He looked quite ferocious, toffee-coloured he seemed to be a cross between a pit bull and a basset hound. He had legs as bowed as a Queen

Anne chair, a few yellowing teeth and always appeared to have an enormous smile on his face. His tongue perpetually lolling from one side of his mouth and a constantly wagging tail. His eyes were a little cloudy with a blue film covering the centre of each. We made him a comfortable bed in the shed because he refused to set foot in the house and I wasn't about to make him do anything he didn't want to. We gradually got to know each other, he even let me stroke his head, although he always remained seemingly aloof. What we did not realize until later was that he was totally deaf.

His owner turned up about a month later to claim him and told us of her regret that they had left in such a hurry they had forgotten about him. Bodger carried the scars of their ownership around his neck where his chain had chaffed and hair wouldn't grow. Ilija flatly refused to return him until the women reappeared later in the day with a little boy who said it was his dog and please would we give him back. Ilija and I felt guilty and so we drove them home with Bodger in the back of the car. On arrival, we all went into the owner's garden. Bodger looked around once or twice ambled over to the open gate and ran off. He was back at our house before us waiting outside our front door. His owner's response was a terse 'Keep him he's useless anyway'. Bodger lived out his life with us, learnt to live indoors and answered commands if tapped on the shoulder. He eventually went blind too but lived to the magnificent age of 19.

We had many experiences with homeless animals. Cats came to stay for days, weeks or sometimes years, I just fed those that came with whatever I had. Later, we took in a tiny, nine-day-old, German Shepherd puppy we called Dona, short for Maradona because she loved to play football. Her mother was an ex-army security dog and so was her sire. Before they left for Serbia, there had been an Army dog unit stationed in the town. It had been a renowned breeding centre for specialist dogs. When they left at the beginning of the conflict, one of the handlers stayed behind with his dog, the mother of Dona. She had a litter of 11 puppies and when they were nine days old the postman failed to close the garden gate and Dona's dam was run over and killed by a lorry. The call went out to anyone who was willing to take one of the pups to collect it immediately. We chose Dona because, in spite of the fact that her eyes were barely open, she ran out to greet us. Ilija carried her home inside his uniform tunic and it was love at first sight for both of them. She was fed every two hours on mixture of warm milk, water, yeast and sunflower oil. She had her bed under a low, coffee table where she felt safe. We were always to regret that decision because even as a full-grown, large and powerful dog she always tried to get under coffee tables! She lived for 14 years and her world revolved entirely around Ilija. She awaited his return and could hear the car coming from several hundred metres away. When he left the house, she fretted and sulked until he returned and no amount of attempted bribery helped. She tolerated me, allowed me to pet her, bathe and feed her, but that was it. Her heart belonged to daddy. She loved the cats and Bodger but had a life-long antipathy to postmen or policemen, however, those wearing camouflage fatigues, like Ilija, were acceptable.

I was alone in our house one evening during that winter of 1992 when, as usual, the only people at home in the evening, in our street, were women or elderly men. I heard my neighbour Dushanka calling me from the house opposite. I opened a window and she yelled that there were men in our garden. She said she had called the police and that I should stay inside. About twenty minutes later the police came, welooked all around and it was then that I discovered most of our chickens and ducks were missing from their sheds. The police told me again to stay inside and left.

Of course, I knew there was little or nothing they could do. Ilija's tour of duty ended and he came home the next morning. After he had heard my news, he took me outside and said 'Now you will learn to shoot an AK47!' This is a big assault rifle and he taught me to load the ammunition clip, how to put the safety catch on and off and the importance of keeping the safety catch on. How to hold it so that it would be stable and not hurt my shoulder. How to stand with feet apart and look like you meant it. Finally came the moment when aiming up in the air I fired it. 'Open your eyes for goodness sake!' shouted this alien Ilija, now in army instructor mode. I squeezed the trigger again, the same result, eyes shut. 'Where do all these bullets go?' I asked worriedly, wondering if they would come straight down and hit me on the head! 'Well, naturally they will come down, but they will have lost their force and just fall harmlessly to the ground.' He said. Ilija had tried to teach me Aikido during our time in Osijek, and while I had mastered some of the moves I could not master the art of keeping my eyes open. Now Ilija groaned and told me that I couldn't shoot a gun with my eyes closed or I may kill people I am not aiming at. My answer was immediate. 'I am not going to kill anyone because they are stealing ducks and chickens. I am not even going to fire at them.' Ilija's response was to put my personal firearm in the corner of the bedroom by the wardrobe. It stayed there and grew an impressive layer of dust and cobwebs. I would have to rely on Dona, our German Shepherd for protection, Bodger couldn't hear them so he was excused duty. However, I had no intention of putting Dona in danger's way by leaving her outside at night! Fortunately, the thieves never returned.

CHAPTER FIFTEEN

As 1992 ended and I returned to Baranja from England, everything was noticeably better. Some shops had reopened and it was now possible to shop for most groceries. The journey to and from Baranja and England was much more complicated than before. I had to travel by taxi from Baranja, via Serbia to Budapest in Hungary. An early morning flight meant that I always spent the night before in Budapest and I enjoyed exploring this most lovely capital city. The cost of my travel was taking a heavy toll on our bank balance and I began to fear that we would never be able to buy our own home. I didn't think too much about the future. Ilija's mother had a farm where we would be welcome to live if we wished while we built our own home on some land that Ilija had bought in Jagodnjak. Some years later when we were living in Serbia, we found that a Serbian still residing in Croatia was using our land. When Ilija contacted him and asked him to either buy or rent it from us, he laughed derisively knowing that it was unlikely that we could ever return to claim our land. There are other such opportunist thieves. The same problem was encountered by Serbs who had left to live in Serbia. None could obtain a fair price for their homes or farms receiving as little as a 5th of the actual value of their property.

It was always difficult to receive news of loved ones who had left for Croatia. But, despite numerous telephone calls to all the contact numbers Ilija had, nothing could be learned by us about Franjo's whereabouts until 1993. At this time, I had the opportunity to go to Germany, from where I would be able to contact Franjo's family in

Croatia. A friend of ours had asked me to accompany her to Munich where there was an urgently needed donation of medical supplies awaiting collection. Although out of date, they were of use to our clinic in Beli Manastir, which had been making urgent appeals for aid. Our bus was old and uncomfortable and it took over 24 hours to reach Munich via, Hungary, Slovakia, and Austria. We stopped for a break every few hours or so, but I had slept through most of Slovakia. Passing through Bratislava, the town had seemed very grey and dismal, so many concrete buildings and I again slept. We had an unusual experience on the Austrian/German border. My companion was refused entry into Germany and had to leave the bus. She and I stood outside the border crossing with our suitcases. This was a new experience for me, but obviously not for her. She asked the officials for the use of their telephone, made a call and then suggested that we walked into Salzburg and waited in a café there. A short while later a car drove up, we piled in to find two other passengers besides the driver all greeting us warmly and with lots of smiles. We now drove up again to the border control, a different one than before because we were now in a car. The official checked our passports and we sailed through into Germany.

I met many ethnic Serbs and Croatians from Baranja and other parts of Croatia in Munich. They were quite a sad group. Some were professionals working as doctors, or gaining the necessary extra qualifications or training to enable them to follow their profession there. Some worked as domestic or hotel staff and they all lived in tiny apartments in one area of the City. They were obviously saving as much money as they could to send home to their families and lived very frugal lives. I was invited to a slava and it was a strange experience. There were both Orthodox Serbs and their Catholic Croatian friends celebrating together. A newly arrived Serb joined us and made an unpleasant comment about the Croatian State. Immediately the atmosphere changed from one of conviviality to angry exchanges and tremendous tension. We took our leave, these people had moved to Munich before the outbreak of hostilities. Our new arrival had lost his home and members of his family in the conflict, this was too soon for reconciliation. I vowed, after that trip, that I would never undertake such a journey again and I didn't, except that is for the return trip. One of our friends had entrusted me with 9,000 DM, worth about 4,500 € today, to take to his family in Beli Manastir. I was in a quandary as to where to keep it safe because suitcases get lost and I have a terrible habit of leaving my handbag hanging on the back of a chair. I opted for the handbag and kept it hanging across my chest for the whole journey home! There was a peculiar encounter at the main bus station in Munich. Two coaches were parked alongside each other. The destination of one bus was Belgrade, the Serbian capital. The other was bound for Zagreb the Croatian capital. Passengers from these buses eyed each other warily as they awaited departure time. It was so strange to be staring at each other this way.

The return trip was worse than the first. It was high Summer, sweltering and the bus had no air conditioning. My immediate fellow passengers refused to allow the skylights in the roof of the bus to be opened, declaring it would be draughty. I silently cursed them, cursed my decision to travel by bus and tried to sleep my way through the whole journey. Although I would never admit to it, at this time in my life I was such a heavy smoker that I found the prospect of three or four hours between cigarettes intolerable. Shamefully that was why I did everything I could to avoid such journeys or the homes of people who declared that if I wished to smoke, I should go outside. I thought this abominably rude and just stopped visiting them. I think what really motivated me to stop smoking, something I had done since I was 17 years old, was to be required to stand in a caged area in London Heathrow Airport in the corner of the baggage hall. This coupled with enduring the other special smoking cages, which I christened the leper colonies, finally shamed me into stopping. I pride myself nowadays that I would never force any of my guests to stand outside. However, unlike Ilija, who has lost any urge to smoke, even after 10 years of abstinence I inhale deeply whenever I stand next to someone smoking a cigarette!

While I was in Munich, I was able to try to trace Franjo and eventually managed to contact one of his brothers, living in the North of Croatia. He told me the startling news that as soon as Franjo had arrived in Zagreb in December of 1991 he had been arrested. Many Croats, who had not left Baranja for Croatia by the date stipulated by the HDZ regime, were later detained and accused of being traitors. His family had been notified of his arrest but, were seriously concerned for his safety, for, despite their repeated attempts to see him, all visits or contact with him had been denied. Within days of my return to Baranja from Germany, I set off again for England and immediately upon my arrival there I began a campaign of letter writing to one of the most influential daily, national newspapers in London and also to the Serbian lobbyist group that I was contributing information to. The news of his disappearance and family efforts to find him in Croatia appeared in the national newspaper as a half- page spread and attracted significant attention.

Some weeks later, shortly after my return to Baranja, to our great relief, Franjo crossed the border back into Baranja, as part of a prisoner exchange. Ilija brought him to our home where he told us what had happened to him. His appearance was shocking. He was gaunt and drawn and shook as he spoke. This was the second time I had witnessed the fear lining the face of someone who had been subjected to extreme violence and death threats. My feelings were truly indescribable. He asked me if I would listen to his story and somehow make people in England and America aware of it. He was another who firmly believed that if the people in these countries realized what was happening in Croatia, they would somehow punish those responsible. I still have this account which I took down in longhand and which I gave as evidence to the Hague tribunal. Unfortunately is was judged irrelevant and would not be read by the judges as far as I understood from the Hadjic defence counsel. Inexplicably so in my view, since the climate of fear and terror tactics of the HDZ regime had led the Serbs to fight for their independence. This was a clear example of how their own citizens were being treated. He also attested to the treatment of the Serbs detained with him.

Franjo's Fate

Unable to endure the threats and violence against him by some of the recently arrived refugees from Croatia and some local Serbs in December of 1991 Franjo had crossed the border into Hungary. He eventually reached Croatia and headed for its capital of Zagreb. He registered at his local police station and was immediately arrested. Now he was taken directly from Zagreb to Osijek prison. Here he was beaten and verbally abused, called a traitor-scum and told he would soon join his Serbian friends by 'going for a swim in the Drava.' This overt threat was a 2nd World War expression used by the Ustashe referring to the murdered bodies of their Serbian, Croatian, Jewish or Roma prisoners being thrown into the River Drava. Franjo told of how other prisoners in his cell had disappeared, taken away at night, and he had no idea what had happened to them. The probability was that they had been killed. An additional horror for Franjo was that one of his tormentors was a former neighbour from Cheminac, who gave him several savage beatings. All because he had opposed the new right-wing regime and sheltered non-Croats in his farm from the paramilitary Zengi and their terror raids. One morning, one of his captors told him that he was to be part of a prisoner exchange release and would be returned to Baranja. He was handed over to the U.N representatives and taken to Beli Manastir Police Headquarters where Ilija was waiting for him. Ilija had previously been notified by a policeman friend that Franjo was on the prisoner exchange list.

Franjo stayed with us in Beli Manastir until Ilija could ensure that he would be able to live reasonably safely on his own in Cheminac. He wanted desperately to return to his farm and eventually he did. Now a shadow of his former self, he tried to rebuild his life and raise some livestock and plant his crops. He sank into a deep depression and began to drink heavily. He visited us from time to time and when he did, we would talk about the old days. Not in a light-hearted way, but tinged with sadness, regret and often tears for what we had all lost.

As his future was being decided by the men in suits in the West, he told us of his plans to leave because he was afraid of what would happen if Croatia annexed Baranja. Terrified, would perhaps be a more appropriate word to use. Ilija, now working for the UN promised to keep him apprised of any developments and so Franjo continued to live his lonely existence in Cheminac. Finally, Franjo accepted an offer of asylum from Norway and fled there in 1995, where he died aged 57, a tragic victim of the insane ambitions of right-wing extremists. The measure of this man was that although terminally ill from lung cancer, in 2001 he made the difficult journey to Serbia. He did this in order to buy land for some of his former wife's Serbian family to enable them to farm there because by then were living in dire poverty. Some of them had numbered amongst those who had so cruelly abused and stolen from him during the war. He came to see us in Valjevo for the last time and told us of his intention to return to Norway where he said he could die in peace and comfort. The generosity of both the state and people of Norway towards refugees was something Franjo said was quite incredible and for which he was very grateful. He was a remarkable man and greatly missed by those who loved him.

Franjo's story, in many respects, has been repeated over and again amongst the Croatians, Serbians, Hungarians, or Roma. All the people who would not or, could not accept a new order but wanted the federation of Yugoslavia to survive and through that, to continue life in Baranja as it had been before the civil war.

CHAPTER SIXTEEN

There was a strange transition from war to comparative peace in Baranja in early 1993. Everyone had been demobilized and all the uniforms, except for the police, had disappeared. Suddenly a group wearing Red Berets made an appearance in Beli Manastir. Ignoring the local police force, they strutted through the town and used the police headquarters at will. Ilija and his friends had no idea who they were and there was much discussion about their intentions. An incident in one of the local cafes gave everyone cause for concern. A group of these Red Berets entered the café demanding to see the identity cards of all the customers. One of these patrons, an ex-soldier, wore sunglasses and failed to remove them immediately when ordered to do so by one of the Red Berets. He was struck a vicious blow to the face, with the butt of his gun, by the officer in charge of this group of Red Berets. Ilija and his friends now met and discussed what was to be done. By their actions, the Red Berets were seemingly intent on subjugating the population. To achieve what most believed was their real mission; to strip Baranja of any remaining assets that the work of previous corrupt officials and some high-ranking Yugoslav Army officers had missed. They also wondered if this was an attempt to ensure that there would be no resistance from the fighters when Baranja was handed over to Croatia.

Helicopters were circling above our streets and the local police told everyone that the Red Berets had been sent from Serbia to arrest dangerous criminals, at loose in Baranja. Rumours were rife, but no one knew for sure. However, Ilija and all the men who had been part of the fight to save Baranja were not going to allow the Red Berets to terrorize anyone. And so they returned to their homes, where, despite having handed in the majority of their weapons, they had kept side-arms and some automatic weapons. Everyone still believed that the UN would not and could not prevent a Croatian attack if it came, even at this late stage in the negotiations and were unwilling to render themselves defenceless. Nothing in the rhetoric coming from Croatia sent any message of reassurance to the people in Baranja; retribution seemed to be high on their agenda.

The men now armed, waited for a group of 15 Red Berets as they returned from patrolling the town and were walking towards their command centre housed at the police station. Surrounding them, they ordered the berets to drop their weapons. The ex-soldier who had been struck by the officer walked up to him and punched him. Then Jomla stepped forward. He is an extremely brave man who had fought from the very beginning of the conflict and was one of the original fighters. He could have made an excellent career in Hollywood as a double for Rambo for he is tall, fearless, powerfully built and handsome. But, he is also very hard working and could be as gentle as a lamb. Now he stood in front of the Red Beret officer. The other bullies, wearing their Red Berets, paled, as so many bullies do when confronted by brave men. Jomla told him that the ex-fighters wanted to settle this once and for all because no one was going to terrorize the people of Beli Manastir. This officer quickly reassured Jomla that they did not want any trouble or to fight them and after more discussions the Red Berets were allowed to go on their way. However, the problems with these men didn't end there and Ilija and I were to have our own and most unpleasant encounter with them.

We received a telephone call one afternoon from the elderly father of a notorious local petty criminal. He told Ilija that he needed a doctor after being beaten up by some Red Berets. He asked Ilija to bring his car to his home and drive him to the local clinic. I went with Ilija to see if I could help in some way and we reached the man's farm outside the town after a 20-minute drive. There was a man wearing the Red Beret outside the garden gate and he ignored us as we went into the farmhouse. The grandfather was sitting at his table and was bruised and shaken. He was clearly distressed and told us how these Red Berets didn't believe that he didn't know where his younger son was. As we talked the door, suddenly burst open and a group of the Red Berets burst in and ordered all of us outside. They began to threaten but did not strike Ilija and pushed the old man into one of their cars before pushing Ilija and me into the other. As they drove, they were shouting abuse at us. I had said nothing and Ilija, looking very shocked told me that they said they were going to break both his legs and how dare he interfere in their actions.

Arriving at the police headquarters in Beli Manastir they took us into the cell area. Another man no in civilian clothes came into the room and thrust his face into mine, only inches away from me. He began to yell asking me if I knew who he was. I spoke for the first time, heart pounding, knees shaking I said as calmly as I could. 'I am English please stop shouting at me because I don't understand why you are doing it.' He was stunned, stepped away from me and told me now, in a much softer voice, that they had been sent by President Milosevic to arrest all the criminals in Baranja. I replied, quite untruthfully, that I knew President Milosevic and that he was a charming man. I could not imagine him ordering people to beat up old men or terrorize women. I went on to say that I was sending reports to the Serbian lobby in London and also that General Krstich in Novi Sad sanctioned my work.

The aggressive and nameless man who had questioned us left the room and when he came back after a few minutes we were taken upstairs to his office. He offered us an apology and served us coffee, endeavouring to explain that they had a difficult job to do and we should not interfere in any way. In fact, it would be better for all if we stayed at home for the next few weeks. My flesh crawled and I was terrified of this thuggish man. They drove us back to the farm so that we could collect our car. After we had been released Ilija and I hugged each other and it would be fair to say that I found that single experience the worst of all others I had encountered during the war. The fear experienced was commensurate with the visit by the Croatian paramilitaries in Osijek. Ilija was furious and I think that at that moment, although unspoken, we both knew that our time here in Baranja was nearly over and we would have to move on. I now sent a message directly to President Milosevic but never received a reply. I was appealing for some understanding and reassurance for this battered and bruised population of Baranja. The Red Berets were continuing to terrorize people, but not openly and only if they could isolate their targets. This was the second time I had tried to send messages directly to him. The first occasion was before the U.N were deployed and had been to remonstrate with him when I became aware of attacks on the Croatian population in Beli Manastir. He did not acknowledge that message either. We now considered approaching the UN to ask for their help but eventually decided that since this was most unlikely to bring any useful result we would not. We would be risking more problems with the Red Berets who, it was said were monitoring those who went to the UN base. The fact was that both of us, along with most of the population were afraid of this group, not least, because the families knew that their menfolk would fight back if further provoked. Fortunately, the Red Berets suddenly disappeared much to everyone's relief.

When CIVPOL, the civilian police of the UN, were able to make their presence felt it came as a great relief to everyone. By the end of 1993, they were becoming part of our daily lives. As more political agreements were reached, the UN took control of the front lines and the Krajina Army and local defence forces were disarmed and disbanded. CIVPOL, in general, was welcomed by a populace who had disliked the Belgian contingent of UN forces. Many had found them unfriendly and menacing. Sensibilities were deeply offended by the tattoos these troops displayed, such as born to fight, born to kill, born to fuck, when they used the public swimming pool. The swimming pool was a regular family outing for many residents. CIVPOL was like a breath of fresh air. They were courteous, friendly and helpful, a source of comfort to many after such a long period of intimidation and fear. Many countries were represented, but the ones

I remember best were those from Argentina, Kenya, Sweden, and Fiji. The Swedish members seemed to be in positions of command.

There was little work, but most people tried to resume their former careers wherever possible. We were living on an annuity that I had bought in 1991 and what remained of our savings and earnings from our agency work before the war. Ilija discovered that the UN were seeking translators and interpreters and began the long process of job application and interviews. Much to our delight and relief, he was successful and was appointed as an interpreter attached to CIVPOL.

Ilija's job was to accompany them to the villages to listen to complaints or requests for help from the different ethnic communities. Sometimes he went with one of the UN doctors who also made frequent trips to the villages of Baranja. Some Sundays he accompanied Jacque Cline's party who wished to attend church services in the predominately, ethnically Hungarian town of Suza. On several occasions, he even went to Osijek with the CIVPOL and each time I feared for his safety until he returned from the mission. I began to get to know the men he worked for. They were without exception very nice people. The Fijians especially so. They spoke of their beliefs and told us how they went into the local forests to carry out their religious rituals whenever they had free time. They wanted to understand what the fears of the local population were and tried to reassure whenever they could. Towards the end of their tour, they told us that Fiji had many, many unpopulated islands and that they were sure that if any Baranjians would like to emigrate there, they would receive a warm welcome. They were really very sweet and kind. Others I met from Argentina and Kenya also left a lasting, very favourable impression on all that knew them. They brought an air of normality to people's lives and unlike the Belbat had not appeared as a force of occupation.

CHAPTER SEVENTEEN

The previous five or six years of conflict, anguish and fear were behind us. We had been a team, facing things together, supporting each other, loving each other but, what now? We had never discussed marriage, it hadn't seemed important and then one Friday morning in 1995, Ilija had a day off and proposed a trip to Sombor in Serbia because travel restrictions had now been lifted. It was late September and a most wonderful, balmy, autumn day. Winter chills had not yet arrived; we hadn't even had a frost. Leaving Baranja behind, crossing Batina Bridge to the Serbian side without incident, we drove into the pleasant little town of Sombor. I didn't have the urge to do any shopping because I was saving for a spending spree when I returned to England in November. After parking the car, we strolled through the town until turning into a small square; we came upon a horse and carriage. As Ilija signalled to the coachman, he helped me up into the little yellow, open fiacre, similar to those used in Vienna, to carry tourists around the City. Here was another relic of the Austro-Hungarian occupation of bygone days. I was delighted by both the experience and Ilija's thoughtfulness at planning the outing. I had never supposed him to be a great romantic, although for many years he often brought fresh flowers home for me. Sometimes he made me laugh telling me that he had knocked on someone's door and asked if they would allow him to pick some of their beautiful flowers for his wife, which they invariably did!

After a delightful hour spent enjoying the sights as our horse ambled through the streets of the town we alighted and my next surprise was to be a traditional restaurant for our lunch. Being so near to the Danube, fish is the best dish to eat here and we enjoyed their speciality platter of perch and carp. Over lunch, Ilija suddenly asked 'What do you think; would you like to marry me now?' And that was it. I told him that I would, as soon as I returned from England because I wanted to tell my Mother first. I set off for the U.K. again travelling through Serbia and Hungary to fly from Budapest.

It was an arduous journey by car in winter and it's hard to describe the joy I felt as I entered the arrivals hall to be greeted by my Mother and some of my extended family.. Ilija perfectly understood that I had to spend much of my time in the UK and accepted this most unselfishly without complaint. I chose a simple silk, pale pink, two-piece for my wedding and bought shoes and handbag to match. I decided to forego the shopping spree, buying only essentials because we had to save as much as we could for our future move. I did, however, buy shoes and clothes for some of Ilija's family who were in dire need. I was always loaded down with items that had been donated by my family and friends and usually had at least 3 or 4 suitcases. Yugoslavian Airlines had always been very generous and had never charged me extra, but the Hungarian Airlines did. However, their excess baggage charges were reasonable and since the items of clothing and medicines I was carrying were desperately needed by some; I considered the money was well spent. I was always very well organized as regards being met at the airport by one of our friends or family members who had to come alone to collect me because otherwise we could not have fitted all the luggage into their car!

We had planned our wedding for February 10th 1996. However, obtaining the correct paperwork and having the banns read, as required by English Law, proved to be very complicated. Initially, the registrar in Beli Manastir informed us that we would have to obtain the written permission of the U.K. embassy to confirm that Ilija, was an acceptable person for me to marry. I was stunned and made a futile attempt to convince the official that, according to British Law. I could marry whomever I wished. As long as they were free to marry. Contacting the British Embassy in Belgrade I asked them if such a document existed and, of course, as expected, they confirmed that it didn't. However, they advised me that I would have to have the banns read or, publicized in Britain and that we should both return to the UK to do this. This process in the U.K. would form the basis on which, the Embassy could provide me with the documentation they thought was the one requested in Beli Manastir. We both made the trek to the UK again via Hungary and returned triumphantly with our signed documents.

My Embassy, in Belgrade produced a document, which thankfully, the official in Beli Manastir accepted. We met him at his office a week before the date of the nuptials and he asked us which of the two halls available for such ceremonies we would prefer. One held up to 20 people, the other around 200. I immediately opted for the smaller of the two. Neda had told me all about the civil ceremony and what to expect and it was from her that I learnt that in addition to reading out our names, they would also read out our dates of birth, to the assembled throng. I had no intention of informing all our guest of our age difference which, at that time mattered a great deal to me. Everything was now signed sealed and delivered and we thought we were home and dry, when the registrar suddenly, raising his head said 'just a minute, her birth certificate says that she was born in the U.K. But these documents from the British Embassy state she is from Great Britain!.' Ilija patiently explained that the full title was; The United Kingdom of Great Britain and Northern Ireland. We didn't get involved in any explanation of why Northern Ireland was not part of the United Kingdom. The registrar's brow furrowed and asking us to wait he disappeared into his office. He returned and grudgingly told us that all was in order and we should be there, on time, on the 10th February 1996 at 11 a.m.

Two days before the wedding, it began snowing and by the morning of the wedding there were deep drifts. A group of our friends cleared a pathway to the car and accompanied by my kum Dushanka and her husband I was driven to the registry office. A dear friend had lent me a gorgeous full-length mink coat which I quite unashamedly snuggled down into. Ilija, wearing a stylish suit that he had bought in England, presented me with a beautiful bouquet of lilies and we joined our friends in the small room of the registry office. It was extremely crowded and Ilija stood on my left, with another of our male friends on my right. We were virtually shoulder to shoulder with our guests and as the registrar began the ceremony an insanely funny idea, that I could be marrying anyone in the room and would not know it, crossed my mind. Eventually, the register spoke the words I had been waiting for when I knew I had to respond with 'da' meaning yes. 'Da li vi Amanda Hilda Brook pri cistoj svesti prihvatate prisutnoj Iliju Celara za zakonitog muza?' By answering yes, I confirmed that I was sober and in my right mind and accepted Ilija as my lawful husband. Everyone hugged and kissed, I do so love Serbian ceremonies the hugging and kissing are like no other I have ever experienced! We now formed a procession to the restaurant where we were to celebrate our marriage with our friends. A band of musicians accompanied us on our way with much laughter and singing. Outside the restaurant, we were met by tremendous gunfire as the usual firing of weapons began the celebrations. Another Roma band greeted us inside the restaurant and their leader, grinning from ear to ear with shouts of 'where is the bride?' Replying that I was she, he shrugged, asked me if I was sure I was and then began to play the traditional songs that welcome the bride and groom. The reception was spent, dancing, singing and eating. There were no speeches, merely endless toasting of our health. And then after just a few hours, we had to hurry home. Our two dogs Bodger and Dona would wonder why they had been left alone all day and would probably be ravenous! There were cards and telegrams to read and presents to open together and we spent some time reflecting on our day. I was content, I had waited until I had no doubts that this was the future that I wanted. It had been a simple ceremony, neither of us felt nervous; it had seemed the most natural thing in the world to marry each other. The first wild passion of our days in Amsterdam may have cooled a little but the intensity had not

CHAPTER EIGHTEEN

Formalizing our relationship would now make moving to another country far less complicated too. Although, we knew deep down that all was lost and we would all now have to leave. We clung to the insane hope that somehow, at the last, Baranja would not be handed over to the Croatians. In the previous August of 1995, we had seen helicopters flying over Beli Manastir following the Croatian attack on the Serbian civilians in Krajina called Operation Storm. Over 2,000 Serbs had been killed, some by attacks on the fleeing refugees which numbered some 200,000. The hopelessness of their situation now was evident to most people we knew. But most had no idea where they would go and if they did how they would survive because few had friends or family in Serbia. Croatian Yugoslavia was their homeland and yet they could not return. Ilija and I could easily have moved to the U.K. I still had a home there and the move could have been swift and simple. But, Ilija's heart was in this country whatever it was called, and we knew we couldn't subject his mother to such a move. And so we resolved to find a new home in Serbia. But, not too close to Baranja. None of us wanted to sit on the Serbian side of the Danube as spectators to a Croatian Baranja, where we would never be welcome again.

The smaller tragedies now began unfolding, almost without notice. Before Ilija and I left Baranja, we attended funerals of friends who had committed suicide. One group sat and played Russian roulette until one of them died. Another pulled the pin from a grenade, as he stood in his tyre repair garage and died instantly. The garage he had established some 20 years before was also destroyed. Ilija was devastated by the news of all these deaths of men who had fought so bravely. Most people realized that they would have to leave before Croatia took control of the area. They did not trust the Croatians to honour any promises under an amnesty and did not want to live in a society in which they did not have equal rights. Most believed they would be treated as second-class citizens, which was almost entirely due to the rhetoric of Tudjman and his supporters. They were leaving their ancestral homes many, with only the prospect of a refugee camp as a destination. They had to leave without money or job prospects. Middle-aged, as many were, there was only a slender chance of qualifying for a pension in their old age and all this in a country where social services had almost entirely broken down. For Serbia had lost the war and also the peace, they were the vanquished, and now widely condemned as the guilty party. Some were able eventually to sell the property they left behind in Croatia but at a tiny fraction of the real value and certainly not enough to begin again in Serbia.

There was no warm welcome awaiting them there. There was a certain sense of them being to blame for the sanctions which had crippled the Serbian economy and left many of its citizens in such poverty. The Red Cross handed out meagre rations for a few years but after that there was nothing. Serbia reeled under the influx of people from Baranja, Croatia, Bosnia and then Kosovo. Some Bosnian refugees managed to return home after the peace and some even found sponsors from countries like Denmark, enabling them to rebuild their homes. Other countries generously opened their borders, especially Norway, who as a nation, are spoken of very warmly by the people I know who sought refuge there.

It had become increasingly apparent that we would have to leave Baranja sooner rather than later. As we talked to some of our friends about our decision Grandfather Ratkajech made a very moving little speech to us. He asked us to consider staying and now disclosed that he had written a letter to Franjo Tudjman, the President of Croatia. In the letter, he said that he had told Tudjman of how Ilija had aided

Croatian families and requested that he be granted immunity from any prosecution because he had fought against the Croatian State. We didn't have the heart to tell him that we could not possibly trust Tudjman and our fears that Ilija would be killed if he stayed were not fanciful. I took them the priest's robes, Holy Bible and other ancient books from the church's library that Ilija had rescued from their Catholic Church in Beli Manastir after it was the target of an arson attack. I had hoped to return them to the returning priest myself but since that was no longer possible, I asked Grandfather to do it.

Ilija's first suggestion was that we should move to Russia I declined this proposal and also his second good idea which was Bosnia, the land of his forebears. One of the leaders of the Serbian lobby strongly advised us against this because he thought that Bosnia's future was far from settled. We concluded that Serbia was to be our destination because we had to consider our commitment to Ilija's Mother. We asked her if she would like to join us for a new future in Serbia. She told us that despite her years, sadly she was too afraid to stay in Jagodnjak and would leave with us. She had survived the 2nd World War in Bosnia and moved to Baranja during the 1948 land reforms of Tito. Now, like so many other Serbs of her generation she had to leave her home again. One especially difficult separation for her was to leave the family graves she had always tended with such care, including that of her husband, Risto. She had always expected to join him there.

Vida, my mother-in-law, was a remarkable lady. She was firmly tied to the land and cared and tended for it, knew its moods, its needs and celebrated its gifts. She would never eat beef, for, she declared, 'it would be like eating my mother, for the cow is the mother of the family.' She was also deeply religious and observed all the periods of fasting and prayer. Having said that, she accepted me with tremendous kindness and warmth. My abiding memory of her is when she used to walk through the forest, from Jagodnjak to our home in Beli Manastir to visit us. She always brought me an armful of wildflowers or blossom that she had picked on her journey. It was at such times that my thoughts strayed to an English, bluebell wood and how much she would have enjoyed it. She was very supportive of me and once before Ilija and I were married while I was in England, news reached her that one of the women in her village had been showing some interest in Ilija. She went to woman's home, lectured her and we heard no more about it. Barely five feet tall, the eldest and only daughter amongst four younger brothers she had worked hard her entire, adult life. When she did discuss her experiences as a young woman during the 2nd World War, she praised the German occupation forces. She told me that they had protected her village from the excesses of the Croatian Ustashe troops and that they had even given them food during a difficult Winter. Vida had borne 6 children of which five had survived.

We had taken her back to her village in Northern Bosnia in 1988, to visit her brothers and their families. This was only her second visit to the home she had left with her husband, as a young bride, over forty years before. As the roads twisted and turned climbing ever upwards, Vida seemed lost in thought, gazing at the passing scenery, strangely quiet for she always chattered incessantly. As we made our way slowly through a small village, she suddenly shouted at Ilija to stop the car. A young man was leading a cow from a farm gate into the lane. She wound down the window and beckoned for him to come closer. 'You are a member of the family ....? the grandson of ....? She said. The man nodded in surprise. He was in for even more of a surprise now. 'You have kept that animal in the stall too long!' She scolded 'It is too thin, let her graze.' Ilija said 'Mother, please this is not your business!' She quickly replied that indeed it was her business, he should not treat a cow in such a way! The young man, suitably subdued, moved sheepishly away to continue his journey. Vida settled back in her seat, enjoying the admiring glances at her son's new car. We had rented it, but that did not matter to Vida.

When we finally arrived at the scattered settlement of Vida's childhood home an amazing sight greeted me. I have always loved a form of art called Naive. Some of these works picture little houses set right on the peak of a small hill and this was exactly the picture I saw in front of me now! Two of Vida's brothers had farms on two small, adjacent hills and there were similar farms on similar hills all around. Ilija pointed out to me the forest covering the hills further down the little valley as those that had been owned by his paternal grandfather and those generations before him. They had been confiscated under the land reforms of 1947-48. Quite, quite beautiful! Ilija told me that his father never complained about the loss, because many in fact eventually accepted these land reforms, unlike some of the city dwellers, who bitterly resented the loss of some of their property.

We had a wonderful time with Ilija's aunts, uncles and cousins and Vida's face shone with pleasure. We left not realising that we would never return, neither we, nor Vida. The Bosnian war touched this little haven too. One of Vida's nephews was shot by a sniper as he herded his sheep and his mother lost her reason, never leaving his grave. Now both of the little farm's on top of the hill are empty. Vida's brothers and their wives lie in their family graves, while their children and grandchildren moved away, some as far as Australia. Vida accepted the deaths of her brothers with stoicism as an acceptance of the normal order of things. She did not accept the loss of the farming land, in the same way. Vida was tough but never cruel. I remember my first visit to her farm, wandering around the yard, with chickens, geese and ducks squabbling and pecking around our feet. Vida asked me if I liked chicken; well, that is what I thought she meant. I replied that I did and seconds later, after eyeing her flock, she swiftly plucked one from its midst, and walking away, dispatching it in seconds. She motioned me to follow her to learn how to clean it. I didn't exactly 'swoon' but was muttering fervently under my breath, 'sorry little chicken, I am so sorry.' Ilija appeared and taking in the scene at a glance told Vida that we had to visit one of his friends and would return shortly to collect the chicken. I have never learned to kill poultry but did eventually learn how to pluck and eat them. Vida and my mother were countries and cultures apart but shared the same capacity for hard work, nurturing their families and keeping everyone and everything in order when necessary. Not so very different then, after all?

As autumn approached in 1996, we had news from one of our friends who had left to live in the South-Western part of Serbia, in a town called Valjevo. Ilija was not familiar with the area but, our friend told us of its beauty and most importantly, lack of mosquitoes! Baranja is a most beautiful place but is plagued by mosquitos making what is otherwise, an enjoyable evening outside into something of a nightmare. Mosquitos seem to relish certain skin types and mine was one of them! It was impossible to sit outside on warm Summer evenings without suffering from their bites. Those brave souls that do spend their evenings performing a strange sort of slapping dance as they hit various areas of their or their companions bodies!

In late October Ilija and I set off on the long journey to Valjevo, which was to take us some 5 hours. We stayed the night in a local, excellent hotel and met up with Milan, a new friend, who volunteered to show us the town and surrounding countryside. We found our little bit of paradise about 8 km from the Town, in a little valley. Climbing slowly, but steadily, as we left Valjevo we came across an area of variously shaped and sized weekend houses on a hillside. They nestled on a small horseshoe-shaped area, perfectly protected from the wind by the surrounding forest. None were for sale, but after several days of difficult and complicated negotiations, we persuaded someone to sell us a small, two-storied, one bed-roomed house. There was a tiny bathroom, a kitchen and a sitting-room on the ground floor and a single bedroom on the second floor which was reached by an outside staircase. Ilija was extremely dubious about buying it. I didn't want to rent, I wanted a home of our own and I managed to persuade him that once we had established ourselves there, we could buy a bigger house. Besides, all we had left of our savings was around £10,000. This little house would cost us most of that. It had water and electricity and enough land to grow our own vegetables and keep a few chickens!

The area was perfect, not too far from town and set amongst marvellous scenery. Just a short drive away the road rises until, climbing to the very top of the first part of the mountain range, on a clear day Bosnia is visible in the distance. In days of old, the little road snaking along the bottom of the valley was travelled by the traders in salt and gunpowder. They came from the great trading centres of the time, Sarajevo to the West and the port of Dubrovnik in the South-West. These old caravans made their journeys to Nis or Belgrade in Serbia and then on to Istanbul. It was also a route for the silver which was mined in Novo Brdo near Nis. The road almost certainly trod by Roman legions before the invasion and conquest by the Ottomans. During all its history, Serbian folk endeavoured to keep their culture and language despite periods of their history when subjugated by powerful neighbours. According to legend, King Richard the Lionheart of England was ransomed by the Serbian King and nursed back to health in his kingdom. St. George is also a patron saint of some of the Serbian families including Ilija's and is celebrated on the 6th of May.

It had taken us only four days to find and purchase our new home. We now returned to Baranja and I left for England the following week. I had decided to take some treasured possessions back to the U.K. until we were properly settled into the new home. It was only a short visit because I had to return to pack and also to help Ilija's mother pack her possessions. I knew that this would be very difficult for her and it was. She seemed to have shrunk, even smaller than her already tiny frame. Ilija had managed to find a small haulage company who had a large removal lorry and we began the process of leaving by loading all Vida's possessions first. A few days later and we started to pack our belongings. The house was crowded with friends who had all brought food with them and so we left the loading to the men and turned it into a sort of leaving party. I had given away all our livestock to people who were staying for the foreseeable future. I had already given our goats to the Ratkajech family who were grateful for this access to milk for their young boys. We finally said our goodbyes to everyone, handed the keys over to the Red Cross person who had arrived to see us off and Ilija and I went our separate ways. He slept with our belongings that night to guard them and I went to a friend's house to spend the night, with our two dogs. The next morning at around 6 a.m. with his mother sitting between him and the driver, they set off for Valjevo. Ilija told me later how they stopped in the middle of Batina Bridge where he and his Mother had one final glimpse and chance to bid farewell to Baranja. Ilija then went to the rear of the lorry and finally he was now able to throw his remaining firearms into the River Danube. Because, as I have previously said, none had trusted the UN to protect their families in the event of a Croatian attack. He said it was a very strange experience, almost a feeling of nakedness, in rendering himself defenceless

CHAPTER NINETEEN

I had kept the 3 cats hungry, hoping that they would not disappear and fortunately it worked and they had turned up early the next morning outside our house to be fed. I had bought a large wicker hamper on one of my trips to Hungary the previous month and this was to be what the cats would travel in. I only gave them a small meal of dry food because I knew there was no way I would be able to let them out of the hamper during the journey ahead. I had fixed a water container inside which I could fill as required without opening the lid. They certainly wouldn't be happy with me, but it was the best solution I could find. I loaded the three cats, Mommy a tabby, Patch, black and white and our Ginger Tom, into their wicker prison and lifted it onto the back seat of our car. We now had a Ford Sierra Hatchback, which was far roomier than the old Fiat, which had finally expired. Bodger took his place beside the hamper on the back seat and Dona, our German shepherd, jumped up into the rear area as soon as I opened the hatchback.

There wasn't an inch to spare in the car. I had packed what I supposed we would need immediately on our arrival in bags and small boxes, including, of course, food for us and the animals and a large container of fresh water. There were as many bottles of water as I could pack in because the owner of the new house had told us that there was a small problem with the water supply. It was around 8 a.m. before I was ready to leave and was making my tearful farewells to friends and family as well as a couple of the CIVPOL who had turned up to wish us well. Bepi, my driver, arrived. He was a friend of Ilija's and usually a very jolly sort of person. What he was not, was an animal lover. When he had volunteered to be my driver for the journey, we had omitted to mention precisely who, or what, he would be transporting. He climbed into the car without seeing Dona in the rear, stretched out and sleeping peacefully. He did, however, notice Bodger, who was sitting in the back seat, tongue lolling with what seemed to be a perpetual smile spread across his face. The innocuous looking basket next to him did not give away its contents.

Waving goodbye to everyone off, we went - for about five hundred yards. Then Mommy, our tabby cat, started to meow. Bepi glanced at me enquiringly and I said airily, 'don't worry it's just one of the cats in the basket.' He replied that he had promised his wife that he would take me to say goodbye to the family again on our way out of the town and we were going there now. I might have been convinced that this wasn't part of a cunning plan to rid himself of some of the passengers if he hadn't turned the car around and raced off with newly acquired urgency. Or, if he hadn't said that there were lots of dogs and cats Serbia, especially in Valjevo, so why didn't I get some there if I wanted pets? I resolved not to leave the car under any circumstances whatsoever. I strongly suspected that if I did he would let the dogs and cats out of the car and shoo them away. We arrived at his home and I politely declined his offer to go and 'drink some coffee with my wife'- while he sorted the car out. In the event, his wife came to the car, to say farewell and we were soon on our way again. Bepi's face wore a frown and I could definitely smell the plum brandy. Barely a mile further on the cats began to meow a little more insistently now. I wished we had a radio, but we didn't. Neither of us spoke until Bepi suddenly announced that he was going to have to stop every half- hour or so to have a drink. Otherwise, he would not be able to make the journey. The cats eventually went quiet for a while and the atmosphere was a little more relaxed. I had made sandwiches and flasks of coffee for us and so after about an hour we stopped outside a small roadside café. Bepi declined the coffee and went in for some refreshments. I stayed put in the car and started to pray silently, that he wouldn't get too drunk. After a few minutes, he returned and to my relief seemed quite alright.

About three hours into our journey, I was becoming very thirsty. I daren't drink anything in case I needed the lavatory. Apart from an odd protest from the cats and changing of positions from the dogs the journey so far had not been too bad at all. Well, that was my opinion anyway. Bepi's humour had not returned and if anything he was even more morose and barely said a word in reply as I chatted away. We now stopped at a large roadside restaurant because Bepi said he had to use the men's room. I silently thanked God and as soon as he had disappeared from sight, I sprinted for the ladies' room and made it there and back before he had returned. I thought it was time now to walk the dogs and I let Dona out of the car, putting on her lead, I took her for a walk around the car park. She padded around did the business and jumped back into her place in the car without any fuss at all. I now made a very unwise decision to lift our 14-year-old codger, +bodger out and let him wander freely on his own. As soon as his feet hit the ground, he took off running up the main road. I went in hot pursuit as Bepi shouted for me to leave him because the people at the restaurant had just offered a home to all the animals, they loved them, imagine that! And they hadn't even seen any of them up close and personal yet! They would be so happy to care for them!

Dodging the traffic, including some very large lorries, I managed to catch up with a galloping Bodger and grab him. Now, Bodger weighed about 15 kg and when I lifted him up to carry him back to the car, he just went limp. I wrapped my arms around his middle and somehow, half carrying, half- dragging him, managed to reach the car and dump him back in his back seat. He didn't seem at all bothered and settled down again. I heard Bepi again now. My antics had been watched with interest by the patrons and staff sitting at some tables on the terrace of the restaurant. Bepi, speaking loudly, was telling them that I was not even distantly related to him, but my husband was his good friend and that I was English. Sympathetic nods and knowing looks greeted his little speech, which I chose to ignore and returned to my seat to enjoy some coffee and sandwiches.

We had several other stops, but I didn't let the dogs out again. Apart from one period of perhaps ten minutes, when the cats began in earnest to protest at their captivity by growling and yowling, they were well behaved.

Finally, after some 7 hours on the road, we arrived at our new home. Ilija was already there and as I went into the little house, I felt a sudden, overwhelming sense of relief. The previous owner had left us a wood burning stove, which had been lit and we all gathered around it to enjoy some hot soup supplied by one of our new friends. Ilija's mother muttered darkly about living like gypsies, but we knew that she was deeply traumatized by these events. But I never once saw her cry and the next day she went out to visit her new neighbours and soon submerged herself in village life.

Ilija had arranged with one of our new neighbours, storage for the many items that would not fit into our little weekend house of a home. As we began the process of unpacking, I joyfully threw away lots and lots of cardboard boxes. They had held all sorts of items, such as ornaments, a clock and photograph frames. Was I a hoarder? An eccentric who kept the boxes of anything and everything I bought or received as a gift. No of course not. Since we had left our home in Osijek in 1990, all the other places we stayed had been temporary. We lived in a constant state of readiness in case we had to leave in a hurry, so most possessions remained boxed if at all possible. But now, heaven! We once again had 'our own front door'. We could begin the process of making a new life together again. Despite all that we had endured together, some things were certain. We were still in love with each other, still in love with Serbia and still ready to begin again.

Back in 1984, seven years, before the civil war began, a Nato meeting was held in Oslo. Apparently without any clouds on the horizon in Yugoslavia, Henry Kissinger, the American diplomat, predicted that a civil war in Yugoslavia was inevitable and would be a long and bloody affair.

I had often thought of the incongruity of the support by many countries for the break-up of Yugoslavia at a time that they were still celebrating Germany's reunification and Spain was refusing its Basque population autonomy. At home, Scotland, Wales and part of a divided Ireland, were firmly held within Britannia's power. In Yugoslavia had there been different leaders and had there been attempts to allay the fears of the communities to be most affected by such a move, perhaps, there could have been a peaceful resolution. But I doubt this very much. Serbia, unlike the other republics of the federal states that made up Yugoslavia, had a close affiliation with Russia. A shared religion, closely related language and each using the Cyrillic script, there is a very special relationship between the people of Russia and Serbia. I asked Ilija to explain it, but he said that he cannot, it is something from the heart he told me. Was Yugoslavia's loyalty to Russia, through Serbia, the reason for their demise?

Each ethnic group within the federations were doubtless proud of their individual cultures and traditions. Celebrating their music, languages, writers and poets, leaders or heroes and written text such as Cyrillic but without the evil myth of racial purity. It is incomprehensible to me how those claiming to be Christians, as believers that God created man in his own image, can accept and follow such myths as racial superiority or supremacy.

The presentation of 'the facts' as presented by those who destroyed Yugoslavia is so professionally orchestrated it is actually impossible for minnows such as I to submit a different view. But I have tried faithfully to recall all that I saw, all that I felt and all that I heard.

With the passing of time Ilija and I tried to rebuild our lives I sought to fulfill my commitments as a daughter to care for my mother in England. While he worked hard, to establish a small farm, as well as, to care for the eight 'homeless persons' (various stray dogs and cats) that have made their way to our door. We occasionally shared our memories of Baranja but mostly we didn't. In 1999 as the Nato bombers flew low along our valley to bomb Valjevo I did not think things could get any worse. But it did. Vida died in Northern Serbia in her daughter's house. We could neither visit her before her death nor attend her funeral because Nato had blown up the main bridges linking the two areas of the country. Alternative routes were impassable because the roads were jammed with traffic. Over 50 bridges were blown up and much of the infrastructure of the country virtually destroyed.

In 2014, I was asked to give evidence at The Hague before The International war crimes tribunal, where it is perfectly permissible to quote 'hearsay' evidence, without providing a shred of proof. Where the right of Habeas Corpus is ignored in order to bring perpetrators of war crimes to justice. Really?

In 2015 standing alongside Angela Merkel, President Obama declared that no borders could be changed by the use of bombs.

But they were in Yugoslavia because Tito's decision on borders was never internationally recognised? And as previously shown, never in all its history had Baranja been part of a Croatian state.

Then Serbia's borders were changed with bombs and Kosovo was handed to Albania.

As for me, 28 years after seeing a pair of beautiful grey eyes, (which the owner avows are blue) I have no regrets. I wish for everyone the joy of love, the pleasure of knowing Serbian people and the peace and contentment of spending some time amongst them.

But, hauntingly, whenever I see a chardak, it evokes such, sweet yet poignant memories of those times in the days before ethnicity held any significance with regards to racial superiority. Chardaks crammed with cobs of corn, a sign of a plentiful harvest, winter food for their stock and a happy and thankful community who had worked together with their neighbours to prepare their winter store. The saddest sight ever, for me, is to see them standing empty on abandoned farms.

ABOUT THE AUTHOR

Amanda Čelar was born Amanda Walton in 1944 in Market Harborough, Leicestershire in the U.K. She married in 1966 and with her first husband established a successful chain of supermarkets. In 1987, she and her husband separated and Amanda moved to Amsterdam and here met her future second husband, Ilija Čelar. In January 1988, she and Ilija moved to Osijek, Croatia in his native Yugoslavia. Together they opened a trading agency and worked with local and UK companies up until April 16th, 1991 when, in the early hours of the morning, they were forced to flee across the River Drava, to Baranja In London, in 1991, Amanda was invited to join the Serbian lobby. She wrote many articles for Ian Greer and John Kennedy Associates for the lobbyist's campaign. Her protests were against bias and the poor quality of foreign media reports on events in Baranja. She was invited by General Krstic the Commanding General of the J.N.A (Yugoslavian Army) for that region, to attend meetings with the U.N and to film atrocities and damage to civilian houses in Baranja to publicize these events. She also worked to organise aid shipments and donations for Baranja.After the occupation of Baranja by Croatia in 1996, Ilija and Amanda left to live in Valjevo in South-West Serbia. Amanda worked as an English teacher in a local private school from 2001 until her retirement in 2010. She and Ilija live quietly on their little farm, just outside Valjevo. In 2014, Amanda was approached by the counsel for Goran Hadgič and asked to testify at the Hague War Crimes Tribunal for the former Yugoslavia. Her testimony was regarding what she witnessed in Croatia, before, during and after the Civil War. She gave her evidence at the Hague in September 2014.

Printed in Great Britain
by Amazon